Identity Crisis

By Jonathan Cowan

Table of Contents

Copyright

Forward

Does anyone actually read forwards anymore? Probably not, but if you happen to find yourself here—hello. I promise I'll make this quick.

As this book goes to print, the American Church is in the early stages of a Third Great Awakening. At the same time, we also seem to find ourselves in the throes of a national identity crisis. Never has the topic been so prevalent in American culture. Who are we, *really,* as people and as a nation?

Determining our identity remains one of life's fundamental questions, and a topic the Apostle Paul addressed prolifically in his Spirit-inspired epistles. Rich and poor, young and old, every single human being wrestles with the question of identity, and the outcome of this wrestling match has a great bearing on how we choose to live our lives. Without a solid answer to this foundational question, we find ourselves like ships cast adrift on the stormy seas of life. Thankfully, there is hope. A very specific hope. Jesus. Perhaps you've heard of Him?

The Holy Spirit put it much more eloquently in the Book of Hebrews:

"We have this Hope [Jesus] as a sure and steadfast anchor of the soul..." Hebrews 6:19 (brackets mine).

That's exactly what this book is meant to be, an anchor. Or perhaps, more accurately, a guide to finding your anchor. A how-to manual. *Anchoring for Dummies*, if you will. You get the point.

As you read this book, I invite you to fix your eyes on this Jesus, our Beautiful Savior, and to look away from any trials you may currently be experiencing. The next nine chapters come from distilled life experiences. They grew out of real sermons, real counseling sessions, and real conversations. Real people facing challenges in their everyday lives. It's profound, but it's also practical in every sense of the word. We carry our identity with us wherever we go, and it colors all our thoughts and interactions. If you find yourself struggling in this life, then, at the root, it's very likely an identity problem. An *Identity Crisis*, even.

It's about time to get on with the book, so I will step aside and close with this. My one piece of advice? Try not to stress out while you read. This isn't a self-help book, it's a Christ-help book. Just rest and let the Good News wash over you. And as you read, I—like the Apostle Paul—pray that *"the Father of Our Lord Jesus Christ, may give you the Spirit of wisdom and revelation in the knowledge of Him, that the eyes of your understanding may be enlightened..."* (Ephesians 1:17-18).

Godspeed!

Jonathan Lauria
Executive Assistant to the Pastors, Church 316
Editor in Chief, Triumph

Dedication:

This book is dedicated to:

My Lord and Savior Jesus Christ Who has loved me, redeemed me, and blessed me beyond measure. May each page magnify your grace and goodness.

My beautiful Wife Katie, thank you for being my best friend and my faith buddy. You are my grace gift and I live forever grateful that God gave me you. I'll love you forever and always.

Chapter 1: Identity Theft

There I was—feeling lost, feeling empty, feeling like a failure. I hated the deed I'd done and thought my actions defined me. Once again, I found myself lying there on the floor crying, filled with shame and guilt. Same horrible routine as usual, and I truly felt trapped in and bound to sin. I felt completely worthless.

I had just looked at pornography...again. I knew I was addicted, and the habit was wrecking my life. To be quite honest with you, it tortured my soul! I was convinced God was severely disappointed in me. I just *knew* that He was disgusted with me. I mean, He must've been, right? I sure was disgusted with myself.

To make matters worse, I was a born-again Christian at the time—who grew up in church—and was even a Youth Pastor! Can you say, *hypocrite*? Every time I went to pray, read my Bible, and especially whenever I would preach, I felt like a total fraud. Every time I had to "act like a Christian," I felt like I was playing a part. I felt like I was acting like someone I wasn't. After all, I knew who the "real" me was—a disgusting, worthless, decade-long porn addict.

Every time I would give into temptation, I would immediately hit the floor and pray. I'd ask God to please forgive me, to wash me clean again, and would proceed to promise Him that I would never look at that trash again! At the moment I meant what I said, but, deep down, I knew that I'd soon find myself back on the floor, having the same dejected conversation with God.

Eventually, my bondage got so bad that I was convinced God had given up on me. I was sure that when He looked at me, a hopeless porn addict was all He saw. I figured that even He had given up faith that I could ever walk away from my struggles.

Boy, was I *wrong*!

The root problem of my pornography addiction was that, somewhere along the way, I allowed the vice to become my identity. I changed how I saw myself and how I thought of myself. I believed one of the devil's classic lies: that my behavior identified and defined me—a lie I am sure most of us are all too familiar with in our own lives.

There is nothing new under the sun, and the devil used the same vile tactic on Adam and Eve in the Garden of Eden. It's a familiar story, and for our purposes, I want to focus on humanity's first couple's reaction to their own failure. When Adam and Eve ate the forbidden fruit, the Scripture says their eyes were opened and they saw they were naked, so they sewed fig leaves together and hid from God. Soon thereafter God took his usual evening stroll in the Garden but noticed His creations were nowhere to be found. God called out for Adam and the man responded: Adam said:

"I heard your voice and I was afraid because I was naked, and I hid myself" (Genesis 3:10)

When Adam and Eve sinned, the way they saw themselves changed. Their own self-perception was shattered, and they no longer saw themselves covered in the glory with which God had originally clothed them.

But I want you to notice something in this story, God's response in verse 11 is astonishing. The Lord simply says:

*"Who **told you** that you were naked?"* (Genesis 3:11, emphasis mine)

In other words, who have you been talking to? God wanted to know why their self-image had shifted. Isn't that an interesting response from God regarding what Adam and Eve did? The Lord seemed almost indignant. "Naked? That's not what *I said* about you." This passage shows us that God's perspective of Adam and Eve didn't change just because they fell short. What changed was how Adam and Eve saw themselves.

In the proceeding verses, we see the effect that sin would have on humanity and the Earth as a result of Adam and Eve's rebellion. That is, until Jesus came. My dear friend, when our beloved Jesus came, He changed everything! The power sin once held over mankind has been broken. Here's how the book of Romans describes it:

"Therefore, as through one man's offense judgment came to all men, resulting in condemnation, even so through one Man's righteous act the free gift came to

all men, resulting in justification of life. For as by one man's disobedience many were made sinners, so also by one Man's obedience many will be made righteous."

Romans 5:18-19

The major lie that the devil so desperately wants you to believe is that sin still has a stronghold over your life, that sin still defines you. He'll try to equate your transgressions with your identity. Friend, don't believe this lie. Reject his deception. We all make mistakes,[1] we all fall prey to temptation. Though it may feel at times as though the sin you committed defines you, it does not. If you're a believer, if you've accepted Jesus as your Lord and Savior, He and He alone defines you. Jesus prescribes us our identity—our mistakes do not.

When Jesus hung on the cross, He was carrying the full weight of your sin and mine. He was bearing the punishment that our debt required. Jesus became all we once were in our broken, defeated, and fallen state so He could transform us into all He is in His complete, victorious, and risen state. When it comes to your sin compared to His grace, your sin loses every time. You might as well compare a single drop of water to the entire Atlantic Ocean—it's nothing short of laughable!

"But the free gift is not like the offense. For if by the one man's offense many died, much more the grace of God

---

[1] Editor concurs.

and the gift by the grace of the one Man, Jesus Christ, abounded to many."

Romans 5:15

This truth is why the devil fights so hard to keep you in the dark about who God has made you. As long as you believe the lie that you're a no-good sinner suffering under the weight of the devil's schemes, your actions will follow suit.

More often than not, this is a difficult truth for any of us to wrap our heads around. To the human mind, it seems baffling that because of someone else's sacrifice—Jesus and His finished work on the cross—we can enjoy righteousness apart from our own works. This may be hard to grasp, but that doesn't make it any less true.

According to Scripture we clearly see over and over again that Jesus was made to become sin for us. He took on the full weight of sin on our behalf. But how was He able to do this? Did Jesus have to commit sin to take on our sin? Of course not, and just about any Theologian, from the Calvinists to the Catholics, would agree with that. Jesus was and is the perfect, spotless, and altogether lovely Lamb of God. So then, how did He become sin? He took it by faith.

Think about that for a moment. Jesus had to receive our sin unto Himself by faith. He became sin apart from His actions. At that moment, He showed us how we are to receive our own righteousness: by faith apart from our works.

"But Pastor Jonathan," your legalistic friend may say, "it sounds like you're giving people a license to sin."

I'm not saying our actions don't matter, but I am saying that our performance is not what dictates our righteousness. This doesn't belittle sin, quite the contrary, this magnifies Jesus and everything He accomplished on the cross. We're not overlooking sin; we're looking unto Him who has called us righteous.

Do we still aim to do the right thing? Of course, but now we act righteously because it's who we are, not something we're trying to become. Simply put, our *why* has changed. Our goal is no longer to impress God, to earn our own righteousness, or to get on God's good side. Because of Jesus, we are permanently on God's good side. No take backs.

The devil will do everything he can to give us the wrong *why.* He wants us to spin our wheels chasing something we already possess through Christ so that we're too distracted to follow the call of God on our lives. A large part of the vision for this book is to help believers get the right *why* and become immune to the devil's devices.

I've seen far too many fellow Christians stuck in a life of wondering, hoping that one day they'll be good enough to get into Heaven. Friend, because of Jesus, not only are you qualified to get in Heaven, but Heaven has already come to dwell inside you. Jesus, the very glory of Heaven, resides in you. He is able to turn your darkest hour into your finest hour. When hope seems lost, Jesus is your living hope.

In the midst of one of my lowest seasons, when I was feeling stuck and doomed to be addicted to porn for the rest of my life, God turned on the light for me! I finally saw myself the way Jesus always saw me—through the lens of His crazy grace. It felt like Psalm 18 came to life before my very eyes:

"God, all at once you turned on a floodlight for me! You are my revelation-light in my darkness, and in your brightness I can see the path ahead. With you as my strength I can crush an enemy horde, advancing through every stronghold that stands in front of me."

Psalm 18:28-29 TPT

The switch finally flipped, and I realized who I was in Jesus! I finally understood that my identity wasn't dependent on my own effort or performance. It wasn't about achieving; it was all about receiving. When my heart latched on to my true identity in Christ, everything changed.

I decided to begin calling myself who God called me in His Word: righteous, justified, holy, beloved. Every time I would give into temptation and look at porn, instead of going into a fit of self-deprecation, I would stand up and call myself the righteousness of God in Christ Jesus.

I have to be honest, in the beginning, I felt like the biggest liar on the planet! I had to allow God's Word to be bigger than my feelings. And while it certainly wasn't easy for the first few weeks, I started noticing a difference. Amazingly, the more I began to believe that I was who God said I was, the more I started acting like it. My actions followed my belief. When I finally understood the devil's lies, his tactics stopped working. It took some time to change my way of thinking, but, once it happened, I was set free and delivered from that bondage of addiction. And I haven't looked back since.

My bondage had all started with a subtle suggestion that I wasn't who God said I was. In the enemy's playbook, this is his go-to trick—getting you to believe you're not who God has already declared you to be. The devil's schemes aren't particularly creative, but he is persistent. He comes to steal your identity in Jesus, and once he has convinced you of the lie, he'll never let up. Any time you try to act like you're righteous in Christ, he'll be in your ear calling you a fraud. But these games are nothing new.

The very first temptation recorded in Scripture—to Adam and Eve in the Garden—was actually the exact same thing: a question of their identity. Look at this with me,

"Then the serpent said to the woman, 'You will not surely die. For God knows that in the day you eat of it your eyes will be opened, and you will be like God, knowing good and evil.'"

Genesis 3:4-5

What Adam and Eve failed to remember is that they were already like God. When God created mankind, He made us exactly in His image (see Genesis 1:26).

We were crafted and modeled after Him. So, when Satan was tempting Adam and Eve, it was with something they already had—something the enemy had managed to steal from them. It was identity theft.[2]

---

[2] "Identity theft is *not a joke,* Jim. Millions of people suffer from it every year."

While millions do suffer from someone stealing their natural identity every year, every family in the history of the world has suffered from the spiritual identity theft that took place in the Garden of Eden.

Ironically enough, Adam and Eve lost their identity in an attempt to obtain it, and the mistake didn't just affect them—it forfeited the identity of all mankind. The decision they made in that moment set the ball rolling for a humanity-wide identity crisis, a crisis that is materializing more than ever in our day and age. People can live their entire lives never really knowing who they are. They can spend decades looking for answers, always searching, but never finding. There are few things more frustrating in this life than knowing there must be more but having no idea how to get it.

As for the current state of affairs, the numbers speak for themselves. More than 20% of Gen-Z self-reports as struggling with their sexuality.[3] More than 50% of all marriages now end in divorce.[4] In 2020 alone, more people died from a drug overdose, alcohol poisoning, and suicide than in any other single year in American history.[5] Sexualization among young kids is up across the board, and, in some circles, having children attend drag shows or identify as different breeds of animals is becoming progressively more mainstream. And, with all this, who could forget the divisive state of politics and the increasing global unrest? Yet, in the midst of all this craziness, Church attendance is down in almost all categories.[6] Not only that but, on average, over one thousand men and women are leaving the ministry every month.[7] As a society, these trends are not sustainable.

All these crises are just the fruit of a deeper root issue. They're symptoms of a worldwide identity crisis. My friend, I submit to you that the answer is not more pills, more alcohol, or more sex. The answer is not in more entertainment, a new job, or a new degree The answer is certainly not in winning the approval of others. While they may help temporarily medicate the symptoms, these things are powerless to help you discover your true identity and destiny.

The fact of the matter is that the answer to the plaguing question of "Who am I?" can't be found in or of ourselves. When we look within ourselves on some quest for self-discovery, the answers will continue to elude us. We'll remain in confusion and void of confidence. The fundamental questions of identity have nagged at humanity for thousands of years, and, in ourselves, not a lot of progress has been made.

These are big questions, and it takes a big God to answer them. Thankfully, we have just that. As Christians, our identity can only be found in Jesus. Christ is the only answer to our identity crisis.

I believe throughout this book God's Spirit is going to reveal to you who you really are. I believe that, through Him, you're going to take back your identity and stand confident in who He made you to be.

In this life, there will be many ups and downs, but the one thing you can always depend on is the enduring grace of God. You may feel like you're stuck. You may feel like your actions have defined you. You may look at yourself and see an unworthy sinner who brings constant disappointment to Jesus.

My friend, these are all lies, and by the end of this book—as we dive further into the identity we have in Jesus—I believe you'll see yourself in a whole new light. I believe the Spirit of God will cause these pages to come alive and bring you to a place of complete confidence in Jesus. It's time to walk in the victory you were always meant to have!

---

[3] Jones, Jeffrey M. "LGBT Identification in U.S. Ticks Up to 7.1%." *Gallup*. February 17, 2022. [4] Crowley, Jason. "How Many Marriages End in Divorce?" *Survive Divorce*. August 2, 2022. [5] "Pain in the Nation 2022." *Trust for America's Health*. May 24, 2022. [6] Jones, Jeffrey M. "U.S. Church Membership Falls Below Majority for First Time." *Gallup*. March 29, 2021. [7] "Statistics in Ministry." *Pastoral Care, Inc.* Fall 2021.

Chapter 2: A Revelation of Identity

Who am I?

This is a fundamental question of life, one that every single person on the planet will ask themselves. And the sad part is, far too many people will live their entire life never really knowing who they are. They'll spend decades upon decades and hundreds of thousands of dollars trying to find themselves and to no avail. They'll look to people, to their career, to culture, to a dead religion, to education, to money, to friends, and to politicians to tell them who they are.

The problem with looking to something natural to give you an identity is it will always be unstable. It'll be fragile, always up for debate, and subject to change, which inevitably leads to frustrations. My friend, this is not how our Heavenly Father wants us to live our lives. He wants us to know and believe with full confidence that we are who He says we are.

Knowing who you are and Whose you are two of the most important questions to settle in your heart. The more of these truths that you know, the less room there is for deception in your life.

So then, who are we? Who does God say we are? By the grace of God, I believe you'll be able to answer these questions by the end of this book.

Before we can truly understand who we are, we must first know who Jesus is.

Let's look at a passage of scripture from Matthew 16:

"When Jesus came into the region of Caesarea Philippi, He asked His disciples, saying, "Who do men say that I, the Son of Man, am?" So, they said, "Some say John the Baptist, some Elijah, and others Jeremiah or one of the prophets." He said to them, "But who do you say that I am?" Simon Peter answered and said, "You are the Christ, the Son of the living God." Jesus answered and said to him, "Blessed are you, Simon Bar-Jonah, for flesh and blood has not revealed this to you, but My Father who is in heaven."

Matthew 16:13-17

Jesus was asking His disciples the ten-million-dollar question: "Who do *you* say that I am?" There will always be a disconnect in your relationship with Jesus if your approach to Him is based on what others have said about Him rather than who you know Him to be in your heart.

This is what I call the difference between tradition and revelation. A tradition is something that is passed down to you by someone else. I am all for traditions when it comes to family, maybe for a holiday or birthday, but your relationship with God must be founded and grounded on a revelation straight from Heaven.

I believe one big reason so many feel like their relationship with God is empty, powerless, or mundane might be because it's based on the wrong thing—tradition instead of revelation. Tradition drains the power right out of revelation. Jesus said it Himself to a group of Pharisees and teachers of the Law in Mark chapter seven:

"…making the word of God of no effect through your tradition which you have handed down."
Mark 7:13

Now, let's look at an example of revelation. In the Gospel of Matthew, Jesus gathered His disciples and asked them a vital question:

*"When Jesus came into the region of Caesarea Philippi, He asked His disciples, saying, 'Who do men say that I, the Son of Man, am?' So they said, 'Some say John the Baptist, some Elijah, and others Jeremiah or one of the prophets.' He said to them, 'But who do you say that I am?' Simon Peter answered and said, 'You are **the** Christ, **the** Son of the living God'"* (Mathew 16:13-16, emphasis mine)

Peter declared that Jesus is not "one of" anything. He is One of a Kind, He is set apart, and He is above all others. This response was a divine revelation of who Jesus is, and it opened the door for Jesus to then give Peter a revelation of his own personal identity in Christ:

"Blessed are you, Simon Bar-Jonah, for flesh and blood has not revealed *this* to you, but My Father who is in heaven. And I also say to you that **you are Peter, and on this rock I will build My church**, and the gates of Hades shall not prevail against it" (Matthew 16:17-18, emphasis mine).

Once Peter understood who Jesus was, then he was ready to understand himself. You see, the foundation for your identity is knowing who Jesus is. As New Creations in Christ, our identity is completely wrapped up in Jesus. The Bible talks about this all over Scripture, but perhaps nowhere as bluntly as in 1 John 4:17:

"As He is, so are we in this world."

There's a huge difference between knowing something about God and actually knowing God.

As I said in chapter one, I grew up in a Christian home— and as a pastor's kid—so I was no stranger to knowing about God. When I left home to attend Bible School, I slowly began to realize a lot of my relationship with God was based on what people had told me about Him instead of what I knew for myself.

I'm not saying hearing about God is a bad thing, but that is a very fragile foundation for your relationship with Him. You need something sturdier than just what someone else has told you. You need to know Him for yourself because He does desire a personal, intimate relationship with *you.*

So, when I was 20 years old, I moved home and began to seek God out for myself. I told the Lord I wanted to start from nothing and allow His revelation to build me a strong foundation in Him. I wanted to go from knowing information to having a revelation.

As I began getting back to the basics, the Lord showed me what I call the Four Pillars of my belief. Everything I believe about God rests on these four pillars.

Pillar 1 - I believe God exists

As basic as that sounds, it's very important. Hebrews 11:6 says *"Without faith it is impossible to please God, for He who comes to God must believe He is and that He is a Rewarder of those who diligently seek Him."*

Even though I've grown up the son of a preacher, you'd be surprised how often the devil tried to make me doubt the very existence of God, and he uses that tactic on everyone. Even though I never really doubted God's existence in theory, I still wanted to make sure I believed God was real to me personally. I needed to ensure my approach to God was based on my faith in Him, not my parents'.

As I said before, I couldn't just accept that God was real because my dad said so. If I did, that'd be nothing more than a tradition, and that my dear friends is where dead religion gets its start.

The backbone of religion is tradition. Tradition lacks intimacy, but true revelation is an intimate knowing. I needed to begin an intimate knowing of God, and I started with a revelation of His existence.

Pillar 2 - I believe God loves me

This is huge in your walk with God, and to be honest, this is where the identity crisis usually begins. Any step you take in your walk with God that doesn't begin, sustain, and end with God's unconditional, immovable, and illogical love for you is destined to get off track.

Not believing and personalizing the love of God for myself is what kept my faith walk very fragile, and it's what kept me addicted to porn for so long. I would waiver on whether God actually could love someone like me, and, in doing so, fell deeper into bondage.

My biggest block for receiving His love for me came from wrong belief. I based the strength of His love on my current performance rather than looking at how He had already demonstrated His unrelenting love for me.

I feel that there are many reading this book that struggle with the same way of thinking. You know "God so loved the world" but you have a difficult time believing God so loves you.

I know in your heart you want to believe God loves you, but in your head, all you can see are your failings and flaws. My friend, the flaws you have, the mistakes you've made, the sins you've committed, do not shock or surprise your Heavenly Father. Let me show you a powerful passage of Scripture that helped cement this pillar of belief for me:

"For when the time was right, the Anointed One came and died to demonstrate His love for sinners who were entirely helpless, weak, and powerless to save themselves. Now, would anyone dare to die for the sake of a wicked person? We can all understand if someone was willing to die for a truly noble person.
But Christ proved God's passionate love for us by dying in our place while we were still lost and ungodly"
Romans 5:6-8, TPT

Even while we were yet sinners, still warring against God and utterly devoid of any way to repay the great debt that kept us separated away from Him, He came to save us. This very thought, Almighty God stepping into the mess *we* made to close the divide *we* created while never asking for anything in return brings me to tears.

It seems crazy, it seems illogical, it seems reckless, it seems too good to believe, and yet that's exactly what happened.

God, in His obsessive love, came to rescue you from the chains that held you down. God saw you ensnared in bondage and He Himself decided to liberate you. That's amazing love, that's your Heavenly Father.

All of humanity wants to be wanted and longs to be loved. As people, we crave attention and affection, and many of us will go to great lengths to try and be noticed. We may even go so far as to adopt a new identity, pretending to be someone we're not, just to get one person to stop and see us.

With our insatiable desire to be loved, you may pick up habits or traits that aren't natural. These can be small things, like changing your hairstyle, your clothing, etc. These can also be fundamental, life-altering decisions. You may even feel the need to change genders to hopefully, finally find some form of peace and acceptance. My friend, God wants you to know you are already accepted and you can find peace in His love at this very moment.

While it may feel like an oversimplification, the answer to any identity crisis you may be facing is simply the love of your Heavenly Father. His love is what brought me out of feeling like I'd never measure up to living life in fulfillment and basking in the light of His love and grace.

God doesn't want you to be enslaved to any person's validation. Will you allow Him to love you? Will you allow His love to permeate your whole being and envelope your soul right now? His love can restore a shattered heart and heal a hurting soul. It can even redeem the years you may have wasted looking for love in all the wrong places, years that you spent seeking the very love God already has towards you. No one is too far gone. If the Lord did it for me, He can do it for you. You're *not* unlovable, you're *not* damaged. You are the very delight of God's heart, the apple of His eye.

When you start to believe that God really does love you, you'll be able to face this life with confidence and boldness. Knowing God's love allows us to be brave in the face of uncertainty, regardless of the circumstances. Even if you still have some questions about your faith today, believing in His love keeps you grounded while you search for the answers. God is patient, and He is always willing to meet us where we are.

If you get nothing else from this book, please get this: God loves you with an everlasting, never-fading, unconditional, unrelenting, obsessive, passionate love!

Pillar 3 - I believe God is a Good God

The saying is ancient, "God is good, all the time. All the time, God is good." Many say this, much fewer actually believe it. Most people that believe in God believe that all good and evil are caused by God. Even the insurance companies call tornadoes, hurricanes, and other natural disasters "Acts of God," despite the fact these disasters do nothing but kill people and destroy property.

The Bible disagrees with some insurance companies' opinion.[3] God takes no credit for these sorts of disasters. Scripture makes this clear in John 10:10:

"The thief does not come except to steal, kill, and destroy. But I have come that they may have life and have it more abundantly."

In this scripture, Jesus gives us a clear separation between Who He is and what He does versus who the devil (the thief) is and what he does. Jesus is telling us wherever you see stealing, killing, or destroying, I want you to know that I'm not in it.

That's the tactic of the devil, to do evil in your life and then blame it on God. The sad part is, that tactic works all too often. But your Heavenly Father wants only to bring good in your life.

When God was creating the Earth, He would often look over His creation to ensure it was good. In Genesis 1:31, God surveyed His creation and declared its *goodness*:

"And God saw everything that He had made, and behold, it was very good."

Take a moment to think about all the things God created for us: warm sandy beaches, beautiful mountain ranges, natural sugars (praise His name!), and the joy of connection through community, just to name a few. He even took the time to make puppies! How can you say the same God who gave us Golden Retrievers

---

[3] Sorry, Jake.

isn't into things being good? But, through the fall of man, the enemy took what God made good and did his best to pervert it, to somehow find the bad in it and bring it to the surface.

But to show you once again just how good God is, He redeemed us, through His grace and mercy, and reconciled us back to Himself. Now, we are free to experience His goodness once again. From the very moment Adam and Eve sinned, the Lord put a plan in motion to redeem us. He rescued our lives from the perversion of the enemy so we could have "life more abundantly," the same type of life Jesus preached. .

God's priority in both creation and redemption was to ensure that everything was good—and that's still His priority for you today. He wants your life to be saturated with His goodness.

Pillar 4 - I believe God loves people

We've already established that God so loves me, but it's vitally important we never forget that God also loves people (difficult as they may be).

Some joke that it would be easy to be a Christian and walk in love if it wasn't for other people. Honestly, they probably have a point, but that doesn't change the fact that even in our undeserving state, God still loved us enough to give His best Gift, Jesus, to die in our stead.

"While we were yet sinners, Christ died for us," and all that good stuff.

Yes, people may be difficult sometimes, but we can rely on the strength of God inside us to show them a better way and love them through the difficulty. Jesus did it, and by His grace, we can too.

God gave me these Four Pillars to be a foundation for everything I've come to know and believe about Him. It just makes things simple for me. For each pillar, I searched God's Word to find a Scriptural basis. I wanted to make sure that these weren't just my ideas but were principles rooted in truth.

Perhaps just as importantly, these Four Pillars also act as a filter for anything that is told to me about God. For instance, when someone says, "God puts disease on someone to teach them something." I take that and filter it through my pillars, those four things I believe to be the absolute truth about God. Since God is a Good God, how could He put something evil on their body? If He loves them, why would He want to harm them? During one of His sermons, Jesus told the crowd that if even they "being evil," know how to give good things to their children, doesn't God at least know how to do the same? (Matthew 7:11-12)

If God really is trying to teach a lesson through sickness and disease, then why do we try our best naturally to get rid of His lesson? Something doesn't sit right with this—and it doesn't match what I know to be fundamentally true about God.

My friend, I want to say this emphatically: God does not want you sick, and He will *never use* sickness, disease, poverty, lack, or pain to humble you or teach you a lesson. That doesn't mean God can't take what the enemy has meant for your harm and turn it for your good, but make no mistake about it, any trace of evil in your life did not originate from Him.

God is a good Father and it's His joy, His delight, and His pleasure to love you and pour out His overwhelming goodness on your life.

You see, having a strong foundation in these pillars made it easier for me to recognize and reject the enemy's subtle suggestions of doubt. After establishing my Four Pillars, I developed a revelation of who God was to me, and I also noticed something else. I finally began to see who I truly was as well.

I want to take another look at our Scripture passage from the beginning of the chapter where Peter received a divine revelation of Who Jesus is. Something special happened at that moment for Peter, even beyond the revelation he had of Jesus. What Peter didn't realize at the moment was that the revelation of who Jesus is became the foundation for who Peter was. We quoted it before, but it's worth digging into again. Jesus looked at Peter and said:

"Blessed are you, Simon Bar-Jonah! For flesh and blood did not reveal this to you, but My Father who is in Heaven." Then Jesus continued with this, *"And I tell you, you are Peter, and on this rock I will build my church, and the gates of hell shall not prevail against it"* (Matthew 16:17-18).

The revelation of who Jesus is was the open door for Jesus to reveal to Peter who he was. When Jesus said, *"...on this rock I will build my church..."* He's not talking about a rock they happened to be sitting on at that moment, he's not even talking about Peter. He's talking about that divine revelation Peter just had of Jesus. It's the rock of revelation concerning who Jesus is that His church is built on. That's why the gates of hell can't and won't prevail against the church, because we're built on the solid rock of revelation of our Lord Jesus.

The more revelation you have of who Jesus is, who you are in Jesus, and what you have in Jesus, the less room there is for the enemy to deceive you. Revelation will act as a blockade against deception.

My friend, if you're currently struggling with an identity crisis, unsure of who you are, can I suggest taking some time to ask God to reveal Himself to you? I promise that as you begin to see more of who God is, you'll quickly begin to see more clearly who you are.

Chapter 3: Established

One of the major roots of the identity crisis humanity is facing today stems from the fact that we have tried to identify ourselves. We identify as _____, you fill in the blank. But the big problem with identifying ourselves is that we'll inevitably end up basing our identity on our feelings.

Feelings aren't inherently bad, but they change—a lot which can leave you feeling confused. Trying to establish our entire identity on how we may feel in a given moment is dangerous. It's like a house of cards, one small gust of wind can bring the entire thing crumbling down—and life can get pretty windy. Here's how I like to put it: feelings are great passengers but make terrible drivers. If left in the driver's seat of your life for too long, they'll end up driving you over the edge of a cliff.

Now don't get me wrong, we should not discount our feelings altogether. After all, God created our feelings. Your soul—your mind, will, and emotions (or feelings), are one-third of who you are as a person. So yes, they are important, but they are also fragile and fleeting. They aren't stable enough to carry our entire identity. We need something stronger, steadier, and more reliable to be the foundation for who and what we are. My friend, that's where Jesus and His Word come in— He will never falter.

The Bible tells us in Hebrews 13:8 that *"Jesus Christ is the same yesterday, today and forever."*

It also says in 2 Corinthians 4:18 that *"We don't look at the things which are seen, but at the things which are not seen. For the things which are seen are temporary, but the things which are not seen are eternal."*

Those verses give me confidence that I can receive my identity from Jesus and rest assured that it's secure—eternally secure.

My friend, just as we can't look to our own feelings for our identity, it's also vital that we don't look to other people. If we allow the opinions of others to shape who we are, that will keep us riding a roller coaster of emotions and breed insecurity in our lives. Looking to anyone other than Jesus to identify us is a recipe for confusion. Your Heavenly Father deeply desires for you to be established in the identity He has made available. I firmly believe it saddens the heart of God when we set out to be "self-made" men and "self-made" women.

God can only be for us what we allow Him to be. This is why you can have two Christians who both genuinely love the Lord experience drastically different things in this life, some good and some bad. Through a flawed belief system, well-meaning believers can accidentally stop themselves from living in the fullness of God's goodness. We all serve the same Jesus, but we don't necessarily see the same things in Jesus.

Here's what I mean, if I don't see Jesus as my Healer, I have to try to find healing outside of Him. If I don't see Jesus as my comforter, I have to try and find comfort outside of Him. Whatever I don't see Jesus as for me, I have to try and find apart from Him. That doesn't mean God is unable or unwilling to be those things for me, just that someone or something else has already filled those roles. When I choose a counterfeit solution, something besides Jesus, I block Him from being my healer, provider, comforter, and a myriad of other good things that He wants to be in my life.

This could be a big reason why many of us aren't experiencing the fullness of God because we aren't allowing Him to be God.

Going back to the Garden of Eden for a moment, when Adam and Eve ate the forbidden fruit, humanity forfeited their original high position and had to start earning their relationship with God. We see this reality in full display when God eventually hands down the Law to Moses in Exodus. When you look at the verbiage in the Mosaic Law, it was full of possibilities and potential, but came with absolutely no guarantees. Could Israel be blessed under the Law? Sure, but it was all dependent on their good behavior. The Law set a high standard of living, a standard that humanity soon found out was impossible to uphold apart from God's mercy.

The Law read kind of like a contract. It was full of God saying "If you do this, then I'll do this." From the moment the Law was established, what you received from God was all about whether you had upheld your end of the bargain.

This arrangement made it impossible for man to truly have a fruitful and intimate relationship with God. We could never meet the standard the Law demanded—which was indeed the point from the beginning.
God's purpose in giving the Law was for us to come to the end of ourselves and realize we need a Savior. And being the astonishingly good God that He is, He gave us that Savior.

Jesus was the perfect Lamb of God. He kept and fulfilled the Law for us. He came to identify with us, to become what we were so that we could find a new identity in Him.

Scripture lays this out beautifully in Hebrews 4:15, *"For we do not have a High Priest who cannot sympathize with our weaknesses, but was in all points tempted as we are, yet without sin."*

He became what we were—not to pity us—but to redeem us and make a way for us to be righteous and reconciled back unto God.

The Bible also says in 2 Corinthians 5:21 that *"He made Him who knew no sin to be sin for us, that we might become the righteousness of God in Christ."*

That verse right there tells me that I'm no longer defined by what I do or by my performance. I am primarily identified by my union with Jesus.

This is why we call the Gospel good news! Jesus came to set us free from the bondage of sin and make us alive to righteousness. My Dad, Pastor Tony Cowan, puts this Truth in his own very profound way. He says, "All we are and have now as an inheritance in Jesus is because of substitution and identification."

Think about that. Jesus came and bore the full weight of our sin and took on the full brunt of the curse, all as our substitute. The punishment and condemnation placed on Him were due to our sin, not His. He had to receive all that sin unto Himself to pay the price for it. How did He do that? By faith. Our beautiful Jesus *by faith* took our sin without committing sin Himself. He became our substitute.

Because Jesus took our place and bore the full punishment for sin, we can now identify with all the benefits of His righteousness. That means that we can live as He does. While He was the One who conquered the enemy and finished the work of our redemption, we can live in that same victory every day simply by identifying with Him. Don't believe me? Check out that verse in 1 John again:

*"...as He is, so are we in **this world**"* (1 John 4:17, emphasis mine)

What a revelation! As Jesus is right now, or as I like to say in the South "rat now," so are we. The way God looks at Jesus is the exact same way He looks at you today.

Isn't that what Jesus said when He was teaching His disciples and, by extension us, how to pray? We commonly refer to it as the Lord's Prayer, but it's really our prayer too. After all, didn't Jesus begin the prayer with "Our Father" not just "my Father?" God is Jesus' Father, but He's also your Father. He is not this far-out cosmic being with no idea you even exist—no way!

The Almighty God, the One who created Heaven and Earth, the One Whose name causes demons to tremble, the One who upholds all creation by His Word, is the same God who loves you intimately. His love for you is so personal, the Bible even says that *"He perfects that which concerns [you]"* (Psalm 138:8). God cares about every detail of your life, big and small.

Jesus put it this way in Luke 12:29-30 TPT, *"I repeat: Don't let worry enter your life. Live above the anxious cares about your personal needs. People everywhere seem to worry about making a living, but your Heavenly Father knows your every need and **will take care of you**."* (Emphasis mine)

This is a precious promise from our trustworthy Savior! No matter how great the need and no matter when the need arises, God promises He will get personally involved in supplying. He will use all of Heaven's resources to bring provision to your situation.

Now, let's see how this thread continues in our Lord's Prayer. Jesus continued, *"Your Kingdom come, Your will be done on earth as it is in Heaven."*

One very easy and quick way to determine God's will for your life is to stop and ask, "What is God's will for Jesus?"

Is it God's will for Jesus to be sick? Is it His will that Jesus lives broke, busted, and disgusted? Is it His will for Jesus to wander through life aimlessly, never really knowing who He is? To all of this, the answer is an emphatic *no*! And if it's not His will for Jesus, it's not His will for you.

God greatly desires that you live this life in His fullness. He wants His overwhelming goodness to touch every part of your being. That's why Jesus had to come to establish the New Covenant and our new identity in Him.

Believe me, the devil fights tooth and nail to keep people from knowing who they are in Jesus. The enemy knows that once you have a revelation of your established identity in Christ, he stands no chance against you. Satan's best bet is to keep you guessing about who you are, to keep you wandering through life and wondering how God feels about you. If he can keep you unsure, he can keep you unstable. My friend, I believe that as you continue reading this book—along with the help of the Holy Spirit—that won't be your story any longer.

Understanding your true identity basically has two parts:

1. Knowing what your identity is and all it entails.

2. Knowing where your identity comes from.

In the later chapters, we'll really focus on that former aspect, what all your identity entails. But for right now, I want us to hone in on where it comes from. As we talked about in the last chapter, a revelation of who Jesus is makes way for Him to reveal to us who we are. So, we already know that our identity comes from Jesus and that alone takes off so much of the pressure. God is not looking for you to establish your own identity. He established it for you in Christ when He established the New Covenant.

This is exactly what Hebrews 8 says:

"But now He has obtained a more excellent ministry, inasmuch as He is also Mediator of a better covenant, which was established on better promises" Hebrews 8:6

Take notice of who the Mediator is—it's Jesus. This whole New Covenant was established between God the Father and Jesus. We are the beneficiaries of this New Covenant, but no part of it originated with or is dependent upon us.

My friend, this is good news! Because Jesus became our representative, we're no longer under the "if you, then God will" way of doing things. It's now all about "because of Jesus, God did."

Too many people aren't receiving their new identity in Jesus because they're too busy trying to establish it themselves. They aren't receiving their New Covenant benefits because they're working to try and make things happen on their own. I am happy to announce that, as believers, the work is already done.

Not surprisingly, this can be a big source of frustration for many. They're looking to something within themselves, trying to make something of themselves, when that battle has already been won in Christ.

Remember the last words Jesus spoke before giving up His spirit on the cross? He said, *"It is finished."* What's finished? The work of redemption, the work of salvation, the work to establish this New Covenant, and the identity you now possess because of it. No part of your identity in Jesus is left unfinished.

Have you ever seen a horse-drawn carriage? One of the main ways they motivate the horse to move forward is by dangling a carrot on a stick. No matter how many steps the horse may take toward the carrot, it will always be one step away from actually grabbing it. That horse will never reach what he's aiming for.

That's the same mentality the enemy wants you to have regarding who you are and what you have in Christ. The devil wants to keep you stuck in a never-ending cycle of self-effort, always trying to earn and establish what God already did but never quite measuring up.

This is nothing new, it even happened to a few of the churches that Paul wrote to in the New Testament. There's one Epistle in particular that I find fascinating— Paul's letter to the Roman Church.

The believers in Rome were still attempting to relate to God as though the Old Covenant was still in effect, even after the death, burial, and resurrection of Jesus. The Mosaic Law was really all they had ever known, so they were having a hard time relating to God through grace, or through the New Covenant Jesus established. In the fourth chapter of Romans, Paul tries to help the new believers understand grace by illustrating how Abraham, our "Father in the Faith," related to God.

In verse 3 Paul writes, *"Abraham believed God and it was accounted to Him as righteousness..."*

Abraham was made righteous by God through his faith in God. It wasn't by his pristine performance. In fact, he made several mistakes while trying to follow God. The covenant God made with Abraham was never based on dos and don'ts, but rather on relationship. In Scripture, we see that God swore to bless Abraham and increase him. There were no requirements, no "if you perform, then I'll bless you." It was based entirely on God's faithful Word, even in spite of Abraham's unreliable performance.

In effect, Paul was saying, "I need to take you guys back to a time when the Law didn't determine right standing." All the Church of Rome could see in their present state was how they could try to earn God's favor and righteousness by keeping the Law. They were trying to connect with a New Covenant God using an Old Covenant game plan—this simply does not work. Jesus has changed the whole focus and foundation of our faith.

People may say, "Well, God doesn't change." That's true—but *we* have changed—and how we relate to God has changed as well. See, the Old Covenant of Law was focused on our sins. The New Covenant of Grace focuses on our Savior, Jesus. His finished work has become the basis of our righteousness.

And before someone writes to me with the usual trope that this sort of theology somehow "belittles sin," let me stop you right there. My friend, sin was no small issue. It was a big deal! After all, it cost Jesus His life, did it not? I'm not downplaying the problem of sin, but I am magnifying the solution of Jesus. When you catch a glimpse of the magnitude of God's grace, any sin you've ever committed seems minuscule by comparison. Let me prove it to you:

"Now, there is no comparison between Adam's transgression and the gracious gift that we experience. For the magnitude of the gift far outweighs the crime. It's true that many died because of one man's transgression, but how much greater will God's grace and his gracious gift of acceptance overflow to many because of what one man, Jesus, the Messiah, did for us! And this free-flowing gift imparts to us much more

than what was given to us through the one who sinned. For because of one transgression, we are all facing a death sentence with a verdict of "Guilty!" But this gracious gift leaves us free from our many failures and brings us into the perfect righteousness of God— acquitted with the words "Not guilty!" Death once held us in its grip, and by the blunder of one man, death reigned as king over humanity. But now, how much more are we held in the grip of grace and continue reigning as kings in

life, enjoying our regal freedom through the gift of perfect righteousness in the one and only Jesus, the Messiah! In other words, just as condemnation came upon all people through one transgression, so through one righteous act of Jesus' sacrifice, the perfect righteousness that makes us right with God and leads us to a victorious life is now available to all. One man's disobedience opened the door for all humanity to become sinners. So also one man's obedience opened the door for many to be made perfectly right with God and acceptable to him."

Romans 5:15-19 TPT

Paul's words, not mine. And what a glorious, liberating revelation given to him by the Holy Spirit! While our sins were a debt we could never repay ourselves, Jesus' blood became an *overpayment.*

Does that mean we can do whatever we want without consequences or that we now have some sort of license to sin? No. That's a special kind of ignorance, the same kind that Paul had to deal with in his day, and what I've heard one present-day minister call "ignorance gone to seed." What I am saying is exactly what Scripture says that your works are no longer what define or identify you.

People don't need a license to sin. Humanity has been sinning without a license since the Garden of Eden, and, frankly, we've become pretty good at it. What we do need, however, is a way out of sin. Let me put it to you this way: because of the finished work of Jesus, grace is not a license *to sin* but a license for your identity *to never be touched* or altered by sin.

Am I saying that we really are who God says we are, even apart from our works? Yes, that's exactly what I'm saying. Let me bring this back to the foundation, did Jesus have to commit sin to become sin for you? Absolutely not! As we discussed earlier, He was the perfect, spotless Lamb of God—completely without blame. He had to receive humanity's sin identity by faith. This principle is the same reason that you and I can enjoy this wonderful New Covenant, we receive all we are in Christ by faith. We are simply walking in the other side of Jesus' sacrifice on the cross, becoming righteous by faith, apart from our own works.

This, my friends, is what God desires for your heart to be established on. He wants your whole life to rest on His finished work of redemption, to rest on His righteousness. He wants you to be grounded in the faithfulness of Jesus. God's Word sums this up best in the book of Colossians:

"As you therefore have received Christ Jesus the Lord, so walk in Him, rooted and built up in Him and established in the faith, as you have been taught, abounding in it with thanksgiving" (Colossians 2:6-7).

Notice how verse 6 begins, it says "As you therefore have received Christ Jesus the Lord, so walk in Him..." I ask you, how did you receive Jesus? It was by grace through faith. We didn't earn Him, we didn't deserve Him, we just received Him as a Gift.

Don't establish your life and your relationship with God on the basis of earning, establish it on the basis of receiving. Let Jesus be your Rock, your Foundation, let Him be what you're rooted in. It'll keep you solid, stable, and secure. I can assure you, both from the Word of God and from personal experience, when you cement your life and your identity on the foundation of Jesus, you'll find that you have unshakable confidence and unquestionable peace. Regardless of what changes and challenges come your way, you'll be firmly fixed on Him through it all. Jesus is our firm foundation!

Chapter 4: Who God Says I Am

Smith Wigglesworth, a man who God used mightily in the early 20th century, said this: "You must come to see how wonderful you are in God and how helpless you are in yourself."

In my life, I have heard many people say many different things about me. A few years back, I received an email that completely blasted me. The author of this message felt the need to tell me "who I really was" by spewing a bunch of junk over the course of a few paragraphs. They even had the nerve to say, "what people should really know about you is this…" Believe me when I say that I got so angry! I wanted to lash out and write back to let them know who I thought *they* were. If they wrote four paragraphs, then I'd write five. I remember calling my brother and telling him to speak faith to me because I was about to lose it!

After a few minutes of talking with him, I came to realize that this would be a defining moment for me. I had a choice to make. Would I allow someone else to identify me? Would I allow their opinion to dictate who I was and how I was going to act? Or would I choose to hold my peace and stand confident in who God already told me I was?

In case you're wondering, I chose not to respond and did not allow their words to shake me.

That was not the first nor the last time something like that happened to me. In this life, you will always have people who want to try and identify you. They take it upon themselves to slap a label on you and attempt to shake your confidence.

I'm sure most of us are familiar with the phrase "Sticks and stones may break my bones, but words will never hurt me." While that phrase sounds nice in theory, it couldn't be further from the truth.

When someone calls you something contrary to who God has called you, stop answering to that name. If someone calls you sick, don't answer. If they call you poor, don't answer. If they call you dense and dumb, don't answer. These names can only shake and hurt us if we don't understand the truth regarding what God has already called us. If we know God's opinion of us, these curses will bounce right off.

Words are powerful. In Hebrews 11:3 it says, *"the world was created by the Word of God."* In Genesis chapter 1, when God saw the darkness, He spoke to the darkness and commanded *"Light be! And light was."* Words are so powerful that they actually created and continue to uphold the very world we live in.

By the same token, when God speaks over you through His Spirit and His Word, there's enough power behind it to change who you were into who He's called you to be. His words can go beyond your own feelings, beyond what others say about you, and beyond any obstacle in life that may scream for your attention. Knowing who God says you are, knowing what He says you have, and knowing what He says you can do will help you tune out every voice of doubt in your life.

It's the devil's strategy to make you doubt what God has spoken over you and to keep you confused about your identity. He hates you and he hates the Jesus in you. Having a revelation of who you are in Christ makes you a major threat to the kingdom of darkness.

There are one hundred and thirty-two different times in the New Testament where the verbiage "In Christ," "In Him," "In Whom," or something similar appears. I believe God wanted us to firmly grasp and never again question who we are in Him—both who He has called us and the inheritance He has given us.

We can't overlook those simple words. They are some of the most powerful words ever to be spoken, written, or printed. As I mentioned in chapter one, it was this revelation that caused me to overcome an addiction to pornography. For years, the devil used shame and condemnation to silence the voice of the Lord in my life. The enemy had caused me to shift my focus off of Jesus and who He says I am and onto my own failures and sins.

I hate the devil! He is the one who tempts you to sin and then puts 100% of the blame back on you. He uses guilt, shame, and condemnation to tell you that who you are is based on what you do. I know from personal experience that the devil also specializes in the bondage of addiction. It's all too easy to let addiction define you because the shame that comes with it is impossible to silence with your words alone.

Back when I was still in the bondage of a porn addiction, I fully believed I was scum, that I was a disgusting person because of the things I did. To make myself feel better, I would pray and plead with God. I would make promises to God in my flesh that I could never keep. I told God at least a hundred times that I would never do that again. And as time went on, the promises I made got more and more strict, as if I could change an inward condition through an outward solution. Let me save you some time, that does not work. I promise.

The real problem was that I didn't actually believe that I was who God made me. Wrong believing produces wrong thinking. Wrong thinking produces the wrong seeds being sown in your heart. The wrong seeds being sown in your heart will produce the wrong harvest in your life.

We must begin to see ourselves as New Creations in Christ. That's where the power to overcome and experience true change is—knowing who you are and Whose you are. It's understanding your old identity, who you used to be, is gone and done away with under the New Covenant of grace, look at this scripture found in Galatians 2:

"My old identity has been co-crucified with Christ and no longer lives. And now the essence of this new life is no longer mine, for the Anointed One lives His life through me—we live in union as one! My life is empowered by the faith of the Son of God who loves me so much that He gave Himself for me, dispensing His life into mine!"

Galatians 2:20, TPT

Your old identity was crucified and died with Christ. When you accept Jesus as your Lord and Savior, you're not just a changed person, you're an entirely new person.

That means when the devil comes to remind you of your past, to try and attach who you used to be to your new identity today, you can reject and resist those thoughts. Refuse to believe the lie that you are anything other than who God said you are. As far as the Lord is concerned, the old, sinful you no longer exists.

Too many believers who have been made New Creations in Christ are still thinking, walking, and talking as though they are stuck in their old identity. We have to stop receiving things we should be resisting, and begin resisting lies the enemy wants us to believe. Settle in your heart that your identity comes only from the Lord.

Never allow anyone or anything besides Jesus to identify you. Don't allow friends or family, society or culture, politicians or governments to label you and tell you who you are. Just about everyone in this life will have an opinion on the subject of you. That's alright, they can have an opinion. Just remember, their right to an opinion doesn't make their opinion right. Truth always trumps opinions.

David faced this same challenge right before he went to slay Goliath. When David arrived on the battlefield to bring food and supplies to his brothers, he couldn't help but notice a nine to twelve feet tall soldier threatening the Armies of Israel. The guy kind of stood out. As Israel's mightiest warriors cowered in fear, David became indignant. A little shocked by his fellow Israelites' terror and cowardice, this shepherd boy asked a very important question: *"who is this uncircumcised Philistine who defies the armies of the Living God?"* (1 Samuel 17:26). You see, in those days circumcision spoke of Israel's personal covenant with the Living God. David had a revelation of that covenant, and it gave him great confidence and boldness. He saw Goliath not as a threat, but as an opportunity for victory!

Multiple times David asked those around him *"What shall be done for the man who kills this Philistine?"* (1 Samuel 17:27), and it was at the height of this excitement and confidence that his oldest brother, Eliab, got angry at David. He came and said *"Why did you come down here? And with whom have you left those few sheep in the wilderness? I know your pride and the insolence of your heart, for you have come down to see the battle."* 1 Samuel 17:28

First of all, false. We can see from the beginning of the chapter that David came down to the battlefield on assignment from his father, not in pride. It seems that Eliab saw a confidence and boldness in David that he didn't see in himself, and, out of fear and insecurity, decided to reprimand David to make himself feel better. Some things never change, and this sort of behavior still happens far too often in Christian circles. Not surprisingly, this is also a favorite tactic of the devil. When you have a revelation of who you are and what you have in Christ, the enemy will use someone to try and talk you out of it, to get you to doubt it. He wants to intimidate you.

My friend, be on your guard against such devices. Colossians 2:8 in the Passion Translation puts it best:

"Beware that no one distracts you or intimidates you in their attempt to lead you away from Christ's fullness by pretending to be full of wisdom when they're filled with endless arguments of human logic. For they operate with humanistic and clouded judgements based on the mindset of the world system, and not the anointed truths of the Anointed One."

Wow! See, God is warning us to be watchful and on guard against ideas and opinions that are contrary to what the Word says. How should we deal with people who constantly try to weigh us down and intimidate us in their attempt to get us to back off God's promises? Let's look at how David responded.

"And David said, 'What have I done now? Is there not a cause?' Then he turned from him toward another and said the same thing: and these people answered him as the first ones did" (1 Samuel 17:29-30)

David heard Eliab's words of belittlement and chose to ignore them. I love how it says *"he turned from him [Eliab] and toward another..."* This is a perfect example of how we respond to someone trying to label us contrary to what God has already labeled us—turn away from their words and towards His words. The words of God are always *"Life to those that find them and health to all their flesh"* (Proverbs 4:22). They are *"a lamp unto your feet and a light unto your path"* (Psalm 119:105). They must be top priority and final authority in our lives. They will *never* lead us wrong.

Before anyone even has a chance to shake your identity and offer subtle suggestions of doubt, go to the Lord and allow Him and His words to establish who you are. Did you know that even Jesus did this?

Jesus started His ministry with a bang, healing the sick, raising the dead, casting out demons, and preaching the good news everywhere He went. Then in Mark chapter 6, He returned for the first time to His hometown. But this time as He began teaching, people started grumbling. They verbally belittled Him and got offended at Him—so offended that they limited Jesus from doing any mighty work among them (Mark 6:5).

However, Jesus didn't allow their doubt to become His. They may have doubted who He was, but that didn't shake Him or cause Him to question His identity. He stayed strong because He was rooted in the Truth that His Father had already spoken over Him (Mark 1:11).

Rather than being intimidated by man's opinions, it says that Jesus *"marveled at their unbelief"* (Mark 6:6). Jesus was actually amazed at their lack of faith. Throughout your life, there will be people who doubt your anointing, the call God has on you, and the dreams God has given you. They'll have more faith in the impossibility of your calling than in the God Who is empowering you to accomplish it. You don't have to be swayed by their doubts. You don't have to waiver because of their questions. You can move on, shake the dust off your feet, and keep moving.

God will give you a vision and a dream for your life that will always be beyond yourself. I like to say this, if your dream is something you can accomplish without having faith in God, then it's just a good idea and not a God idea.

Now, God-given vision will always attract people who are full of doubt. It's like bugs to an outdoor light. They'll say "You can't do this! I know the family you came from. I know the mistakes you've made. You don't have what it takes. Who do you think you are?"

That's nothing more than the voice of the enemy trying to shake your foundation of faith. The devil loves to belittle God's children because he knows the potential of God's power in them. He has to try to keep you in doubt so the power lies dormant. But when you take God at His Word and activate that power by faith, oh my friend, the devil and all of hell doesn't stand a chance!

Going back to our discussion of Jesus, the saddest part of that story is that Nazareth became the only town in His recorded ministry with no documented miracles. How tragic! Their unbelief didn't stop Jesus from doing miracles, but it did stop the people from receiving them.

The same thing will happen with anyone who doubts the gift God placed in you. They won't stop it, they can't stop it, but they will stop themselves from receiving a blessing from it. The Bible says, "Let God be true and every man a liar" (Romans 3:4). God's Word is true, and no one can stop you from fulfilling God's plan for your life. Many may try, but they will all fail.

God promises this very thing in Isaiah 54:17: *"No weapon formed against you shall prosper, and every tongue which rises against you in judgment you shall condemn."* That means when someone speaks a negative word over you or tries to call you a name that

God never called you, you can reject that label. You're able to stand firm in faith and believe God's Word above anyone else's.

The Great I Am has already declared who you are. His Words, not any other, secure your identity. Your health is not dependent on what season of the year it is. Your wealth is not dependent on your nation's economy or your family's income. All of these things—and your own future—are not dependent on anything except your faith in God's Word.

"But Pastor Jonathan," you might say, "you just don't know what I've been through. You don't know what people have said about me. You don't know the attacks I'm facing from the enemy right now."

You're right, I don't know everything you might be facing right now. But what I do know is that the Word of God is the most powerful agent of change in human history. I know there may be several "weapons" that have been formed and pointed right at you from the devil himself, but you can take God at His Word and know that those weapons cannot and will not succeed in your life.

You can stand firm and fight the good fight of faith. You can enter into rest knowing God is turning everything around for your good and your benefit and your favor.

The only way you'll lose is if you quit, if you pull your faith. My friend, keep your faith in Jesus. Keep your heart, your mind, and your eyes fully fixed on Him.

Count it all joy when you fall into various trials. You're not going under, you're going over. You're not doomed for failure; you're destined for greatness. God, your God, will not fail you. He who promised is faithful to fulfill His promise. The Jesus in you is greater than the enemy that's against you. Hold fast to your confession of faith for with it comes a great reward. You will see the goodness of God in this life.

Don't be afraid and don't let your heart be troubled. The very same God who spoke the earth into existence and defeated all the power of hell is with you. He is on your side. For you and your household, everything will be alright.

Circumstances, opinions of others, and lies from the devil himself don't have the power to override God's Word. To quote the Psalmist, *"Forever O Lord Your Word is settled in Heaven"* (Psalm 119:89). If it's settled in Heaven, let it be settled in your heart today.

You are so much more than average. You were made for more than an ordinary existence. The enemy would love you to believe the lie that you don't deserve the abundant life God has made available for you. Satan wants to tie your destiny to the natural realm. In Christ Jesus, you are so much more than a horoscope, so much more than a personality test. Don't be deceived, my friend. A horoscope doesn't limit what God's grace has provided for you. A personality test doesn't disqualify you from anything God has made available.

Your position in Christ supersedes your personality type and gives you unlimited potential. When you align your belief and your mindset with who He's called you to be, it sets you free from any bondage from the enemy. It'll bring you out from a restricted, confined place and set you in a broad, open place.

So, what are we to do now? Get in the Word. Find out who God says you are. Find out what He says you have. Find out what He says you can do. Establish your identity on and be defined by the incorruptible Word of Christ. At the end of this chapter, I will list several things God says about you, and the labels He's put on you. And then do exactly what Colossians 3:16 (AMPC) says, *"Let the word (spoken by) Christ (the Messiah) have its home [in your hearts and minds] and dwell in you in [all its] richness..."*

Allow His words to come alive in your life, and when the seed of His Word is sown in the garden of your heart, don't allow the enemy to steal it. Guard it, meditate on it, speak it over yourself, and watch how it weaves every area of your life into a beautiful tapestry of God's goodness.

I am who God says I am!

I am Loved - Romans 8:38-39

I am Redeemed - Ephesians 1:7, Galatians 3:13, Colossians 1:14

I am Forgiven - Romans 4:6-8, Colossians 2:13-14

I am a New Creation - 2 Corinthians 5:17

I am Righteous - 2 Corinthians 5:21

I am Healed - 1 Peter 2:24

I am Found in Him - Philippians 3:9

I am a Child of God - Romans 8:16, Galatians 4:7

I am Chosen - 1 Peter 2:9, Ephesians 1:4

I am Anointed - 1 John 2:27

I am Blessed, Prosperous, & Successful - Galatians 3:14, 2 Corinthians 8:9, Ephesians 1:3

I am More than a Conqueror - Romans 8:37, 1 Corinthians 15:57

I am Bold & Confident - Ephesians 3:12, Proverbs 28:1

I am Made in the Image of God - Genesis 1:27

I am Justified - Galatians 2:16, Romans 5:1

I am God's Masterpiece - Ephesians 2:10

I am Complete - Colossians 2:10

While these are just a few of God's promises on our new identity in Jesus, I encourage you to search the scriptures and see for yourself just how amazing you are in Christ.

Chapter 5: Who Do I Think I Am?

"God has privileged us in Christ Jesus to live above the ordinary human plane of life. Those who want to be ordinary and live on a lower plane can do so, but as for me, I will not."

- Smith Wigglesworth

I'm sure most of us are familiar with the phrase "you are what you eat." While I don't know for sure how true that is, I can tell you with 100% certainty that you are what you think. The truth is you are who God says you are, but you will only experience and walk in who you believe you are. Do you align your belief with His Word? Or do you allow your faith to follow the opinions of others?

God is a God of choices. He will never force His will on anyone. He always allows us to choose. Take the Garden of Eden for example. When God placed Adam and Eve in the Garden, He gave them the choice to take Him at His Word or to put their trust in something (or someone) else. Love always gives a choice. True unconditional love never imposes its will and desires on others.

God did the same thing in Deuteronomy 30:19, "I set before you life and death, blessing and cursing; therefore *choose* life…"

God has given you the choice. He has made you in His likeness and His image, with complete access and authority in His Kingdom. How much of that you walk in depends entirely on how much of it you believe to be true.

I grew up with two older brothers, and to be honest, I really don't know how my parents put up with us. They had three boys under the age of five. You can imagine the shenanigans we got into.

Like all brothers, we each took up the responsibility of building character in each other and quickly mastered the art of building thick skin. And boy, did we take our jobs seriously.

From an early age, I can remember my Dad teaching me the importance of not allowing outside opinions or criticism to determine my identity. I would come crying to him when one or both of my brothers said something negative about me. I'd go on and on about how it hurt me, and how they shouldn't say that. He would always stop and ask me one simple question: "Is it true? Is what they said about you true?" My mopey self would reply "No." And that would be the end of it.

Those moments growing up taught me a valuable lesson. Specifically, that people will always have something negative to say, but just because it's said doesn't mean it's true. Instead of allowing what someone else said to shake you, stop and ask yourself what my Dad asked me: "Is it true? Is what they said true?" And if it's not true, why let it bother you and bring you down?

This concept reminds me of the phrase "I know you are but what am I?" The older you get, the less rhetorical this question becomes. People all over the world are desperately trying to find someone who can answer this question and give them identity. My friends, only Jesus can do that.

In my life now, I allow God's Word—what He says about me—to reign supreme both in my heart and in my head. Others can't tear me down because they weren't the ones who built me up. God's Word alone holds the highest authority.

As I've said many times throughout this book, the truth of the matter is beautifully simple: you are who God says you are. His Word trumps every voice of accusation in this world—it is emphatically and eternally true. You are not a product of what you do or what has happened to you. That sort of philosophy is a lie of the enemy to deceive you into believing that your past determines your identity and your future. This could not be further from the truth.

My friend, do not believe these lies! I know many of us may have experienced traumatic things in our lives. The attacks from the devil have been strong and long. I know it can be hard to look in the mirror and not see past hurts and past mistakes staring back. But we can choose a different mirror.

Have you ever been to a fair or carnival? I'm all for a good adrenaline rush, but I have my suspicions of any ride that can be set up, torn down, and relocated in a short amount of time. Though, one thing I do enjoy at the carnival is taking a walk through the mirror house. . While passing through, you see so many different types of mirrors that distort the original image. Some mirrors make you look short, others make you look tall, others make you look about 80 lbs. heavier, and others make you look 80 lbs. lighter.

Imagine with me for a minute if the only mirror you ever saw yourself through was the mirror that made you look 80 lbs. heavier. Think about how distorted your self-image would be. Think about how that would affect your actions. Think about how that would affect your confidence and the way you interact with people. I would venture to say that one mirror would affect your entire world.

While this idea may seem far-fetched in the natural, this is a fairly regular occurrence in spiritual matters. Personally, I look into a mirror several times throughout the day. In the morning, brushing my teeth and fixing my hair, when I get dressed, to make sure my clothes match, and at night when I get ready for bed. Beyond that, I also have to check periodically throughout the day to make sure I have an accurate image of what I look like.

The exact same principle holds true for my Spirit Man. I have to look in the mirror of the Word of God to know what I look like, to know who I am, and to know what I have. If I don't keep Scripture before me as a constant reminder of the Truth, I find it much more difficult to stand firm and remain confident in who the Lord has called me.

Take a look at what James 1:23-25 says:

"If you listen to the Word and don't live out the message you hear, you become like the person who looks in the mirror of the Word to discover the reflection of his face in the beginning. You perceive how God sees you in the mirror of the Word, but then you go out and forget your Divine origin. But those who set their gaze deeply into the perfecting law of liberty are fascinated by and respond to the truth they hear and are strengthened by it - they experience God's blessing in all they do!"

James 1:23-25 TPT

I love the words "gaze deeply" in verse 25! That's not just a passing glance or glimpse. It's a steady, intentional observation. Having that consistent gaze into the mirror of God's Word brings you to a place of confidence in who God says you are; it helps remind you that your identity originated with and flows from Him.

Like the old Hymn says, "Turn your eyes upon Jesus. Look full in His wonderful face. And the things of earth will grow strangely dim in the light of His glory and grace."

The more you look at Jesus, the Word made flesh, the things of the earth just seem to fade away. The old saying is true, "Out of sight, out of mind." That's why we have to watch what we watch and pay attention to what we pay attention to.

In our media-saturated day and age, we are constantly bombarded with outside imaginations and mindsets that contradict the Word of God. The more you feed on these lies, the harder it will be for you to believe what He says about you.

Your faith follows your focus. What you look at is what you will look like. That's why the Bible says to "take every thought captive to the obedience of Christ." When a thought comes into your mind that is against the Word, don't allow that thought to stick around and become a mindset. Take it captive and cast it out in Jesus' name. You can't control every thought that pops into your head, but you can control which thoughts are allowed to stick around, eventually forming into beliefs and mindsets. One minister said it this way, "You can't do anything about the birds flying over your head, but you can stop them from making a nest in your hair."

Let me show you a couple of scriptures that highlight why this is such an important aspect of walking out your identity in Jesus:

"And do not be conformed to this world, but be transformed by the renewing of your mind..."

Romans 12:2

"Stop imitating the ideals and opinions of the culture around you, but be inwardly transformed by the Holy Spirit through a total reformation of how you think."

Romans 12:2 TPT

True transformation happens when you exchange your thoughts for God's thoughts. Now it's important to remember that mind renewal does not *create* who I am in Jesus, it just aligns my thinking with what is already true in the Spirit.

Too many of our mindsets originate in the world or in some kind of man-made religion. Nothing will limit your spiritual growth more than a mind that's out of alignment.

Traditional worldly thoughts tell you to accept sickness and disease as a normal part of life. They tell you that, when you get older, your health and strength have to diminish. That you are condemned to eventually lose energy and mental capacity. My friend, that's not at all what God says about you! But what will you *choose* to believe?

Most voices will tell you that it's not God's will for you to live in abundance and success in every part of life. As vehemently as some may resist the truth of Scripture on the subject, this abundant life even includes finances. However, many religious voices will proclaim that living poor is part and parcel of embracing humility and suffering for Jesus. That struggling to make ends meet is just a normal part of life. However, the Word of God begs to differ. This sort of lack-mentality is not at all what God says about you. But once again, what will you *choose* to believe?

Lies from the world and the religious traditions of men have kept millions upon millions of people from walking in their God-given identity. If this inheritance is available to all sons and daughters of God, why aren't we all experiencing it? Because receiving is a choice, and right believing produces the right kind of receiving. You don't automatically live out God's best for your life—you live out your thought life.

Look at what this verse in the book of Proverbs says.

"For as a man thinks in his heart, so is he."

Proverbs 23:7

People often ask, "How good is God?" He is infinitely good! But in your life, He can only be as good as you believe Him to be. That's why Jesus said repeatedly during his earthly ministry, "So be it unto you according to your faith."

Are you the healed of the Lord? So be it unto you according to your faith.

Are you blessed, prosperous, and successful in Christ? So be it unto you according to your faith.

70

Are you saved, justified, and set apart? So be it unto you according to your faith.

Are you everything God says you are? So be it unto you according to your faith.

Do you have everything God says you can have? So be it unto you according to your faith.

Can you do everything He says you can do? So be it unto you according to your faith.

God wants you to live in the fullness of all that has been made available to you in Christ. But to walk in it, it's going to take faith. It's going to require a change of mind. It's going to demand a new mentality.

Few stories in the Bible showcase this better than the lives of Abraham and Sarah.

Abram and Sarai, later changed to Abraham and Sarah, were unable to conceive a child and remained barren for decades. Yet in the midst of this trial, God gave Abram a promise that not only would he have a son, but that he would become a father of many nations! That promise was given when Abram was 75 and Sarai was 65, well past normal childbearing years by any century's definition. But God's Word never returns void, and that promise did indeed come to pass. However, Isaac wasn't born until about 25 years later. Was God slow in delivering on His promise, or was something else at play in the life of Abram? It appears that a defining moment in the story comes around the 24th year. Let's look at Genesis 15 together:

"After these things the word of the Lord came to Abram in a vision, saying, "Do not be afraid, Abram. I am your shield, your exceedingly great reward. "But Abram said, "Lord God, what will You give me, seeing I go childless, and the heir of my house is Eliezer of Damascus?" Then Abram said, "Look, You have given me no offspring; indeed one born in my house is my heir!" And behold, the word of the Lord came to him, saying, "This one shall not be your heir, but one who will come from your own body shall be your heir." Then He brought him outside and said, "Look now toward heaven, and count the stars if you are able to number them." And He said to him, "So shall your descendants be.""

Genesis 15:1-4

This was a pivotal moment for Abram. In the middle of his discouragement, God called his vision back to the promise.

The passage begins with Abram asking God to come inside his tent, so to speak, and see things from his earthly perspective. "God, I'm childless. Come see my lack. Look at my problem."

Because of discouragement Abram had let go of God's promise and began focusing on his need. As a result, he was now trying to settle with God, trying to negotiate God's promise down to something more "realistic."

This happens far too often in our lives today. The devil thinks he's a businessman. He wants to get you to negotiate and settle for less than God's promises, a tactic he's tried on me many times

I remember this one time in particular. I had been suffering from pounding headaches for a couple of weeks and the enemy came and told me "You know what those headaches really are? A tumor." For obvious reasons, I wasn't ready to accept a lie quite so extreme, so he decided to negotiate. He then said "Well, they must be the start of severe migraines. Better prepare to deal with these for a while." I didn't accept that either. So, he negotiated even further, "Well you're just prone to these kinds of headaches, you must get them off and on. That's at least bearable. At least it's not a tumor, right?"

It sounds silly, but the enemy has been deathly effective with this tactic. He kept negotiating his lie to see what I would accept and believe. He knows that I'll live out what I believe and if he can get me to believe his lie, that's what I'll experience.

His end goal is to get you to stop believing God and His promised Word and start settling. That's a slippery slope. If you settle here, you'll settle there. But when these attacks come, you can do what I did. Stand firm on the Word and refuse to negotiate with the devil. Satan, through his tactics of fear and intimidation, is essentially a terrorist and, to quote President Reagan, "there [should] be no negotiation with terrorists of any kind."[4] This should be just as true in your spiritual life.

When he tries to come to you with his lies, remind the enemy that a settlement has already been reached on the cross at Calvary and it's sealed in the blood of Jesus. It's no longer up for debate. You can rest in full assurance of faith that all of God's promises are yes and amen. They're *not* "maybe so" and "let's hope it happens."

This is exactly what God did with Abram. He brought him right back to His promise. He called him outside of his tent, outside of his problem, and told him to look up and away from his current situation

By telling Abram to count the stars at night and the sand on the shore by day, the Lord was helping to keep his attention and focus constantly on the promise. The stars and the sand served as an around-the-clock reminder that God declared Abram would be a father of many nations.

The story of Abram continues for a few chapters and in Genesis 17, God provides another pivotal moment for the promise: changing Abram's name to Abraham:

No longer shall your name be called Abram, but your name shall be Abraham; for I have made you a

---

[4] https://www.presidency.ucsb.edu/documents/presidential-debate-cleveland

father of many nations. I will make you exceedingly
fruitful; and I will make nations of you..." Genesis
17:5-6

The name Abraham literally means "father of many
nations." That means every time someone called
Abraham's name it reminded him of God's promise. Just
like Abraham, you have been given a new name, a new
label, a new identity from God Himself. You may feel
just like Abram did at the beginning of this story—
frustrated, discouraged, and ready to settle for less
than what God has promised. Let me first encourage
you, my friend. If you feel discouraged and frustrated,
there's an abundance of grace for you. You don't have
to have it all together. Remember what Abram did? He
told God exactly where he was, mess and all. He didn't
approach God with a pretentious faith, pretending to be
somewhere he wasn't.

I heard one minister put it this way, "God will always
meet you where you are, but He can never meet you
where you pretend to be." You don't have to hide your
frustrations from your Heavenly Father. After all, He
already knows what you're thinking and what you're
feeling.

Take your worries and frustrations and put them at the
feet of Jesus. Watch how He'll lovingly and faithfully
remind you of His promises. Watch how His presence
will stir your faith to believe again.

I feel so strong in my spirit to encourage you—don't quit! Don't give up now. I know it may feel hopeless, but He is faithful. I know it feels like you're stuck, but His Word can set you free.

The example of Abraham has become a hallmark of the Christian Faith, and in Romans 4:20-21 the Apostle Paul gives all believers insight into how to have faith like Abraham:

"He [Abraham] did not waver at the promise of God through unbelief, but was strengthened in faith, giving glory to God, and being fully convinced that what He had promised He was also able to perform."

Abraham's faith was strengthened by focusing on the Almighty God who had made the promise. He knew— beyond the smallest shadow of a doubt— that God was faithful and that His Word would prevail over the present circumstances.

I can assure you when you begin to praise and glorify God as Abraham did, you'll find renewed strength for the battle. The devil wants you focused on the natural realm, hoping you will give into discouragement and pull your faith. Praising, glorifying, and magnifying God silences him and his lies.

God is faithful and His promises are true, but just because they are available doesn't mean they are automatic. What has been given by grace must be received by faith. The identity God has given you is sure and certain but it won't be manifested unless and until you activate it by faith.

Once you know what God has said about you, receive it by faith, and hold fast to His Word. I confidently believe that it shall be just as it was spoken to you. This revelation of receiving by grace through faith will change your life—and when it does—the devil won't be able to keep you from a single good thing that your Heavenly Father has in store for you.

Chapter 6: Lasting Security

Insecurity is one of the most prevalent side effects of the identity crisis facing our world today. As human beings, we have an innate drive to find peace and security—but any security found outside of Jesus and His Word is like building a house on sand.

Whether we have realized it or not, our security is actually rooted in our identity. Think about it. When we tie our identity to our money, we find security in the numbers in our bank account. When we tie our identity to education or degrees, we find security in our own pedigree and achievements. When we tie our identity to social status, we find our security in other peoples' praise and approval.

You don't have to live in bondage to these things in an attempt to gain security. You can link your identity to Jesus and His Word, and find eternal security in Him. You don't have to look to other people to tell you who you are. You don't have to wait for anyone else's approval when you have the acceptance and approval of the Most High God.

God loves you and wants you to know it! He is adamant and passionate about showing you His love. In the blood of Jesus, you have complete redemption and a rightful place in God's family. Understanding this truth, and holding onto this revelation with a firm grasp, is the only way to truly rid yourself of insecurity.

Let's get practical for a moment. In my marriage, what if I never told my wife that I love her? What if I never showed her any care or attention? How secure would she feel in our relationship? Would our marriage feel secure to her? No way! It would be a breeding ground for insecurity. She would have no confidence in our relationship.

Confidence and security are only as strong as the foundation they stand on. To provide assurance for my wife in our marriage, I have to demonstrate and vocalize my love for her. By putting words and action behind my love, I can help rid her mind of all doubts and questions.

God did this for us. His love gave us a strong and steady foundation. It's a safe, solid place for us to stand. We can have peace of mind and security of heart-knowing and believing He deeply and affectionately cares for us.

God told us He loves us in His Word, and He demonstrated it by sending Jesus. The proof of our eternal value is in the person of Christ. Let's unpack this some more. If I were to ask you how to measure the value of something, what would you say? You might say it's based on an appraiser's opinion, but that's not entirely correct. The final say on something's worth or value is actually determined by the price that was paid for it.

Let's say you went to a store and bought a new painting for $2,000 dollars. Then I came to your home and questioned you about the painting. I asked where you got it and even brashly asked how much it cost. When you told me the amount, I gasped. "Why on earth would you spend that kind of money on that?" I can even go so far as to hire an art appraiser and have him tell you that you overpaid for the piece. Yet, in the end, neither my opinion nor the appraiser's can actually change the value of that painting to you. You saw the painting, loved it, and bestowed value on it when you paid $2,000 dollars for it. When you handed over the money for the painting, you essentially were saying "it's worth it."

My friend, that's precisely what God the Father did for us. He saw us and said "I'm willing to pay the price for them! They're worth it to me." Other people may have an opinion about your worth and value, but they didn't pay the price for you. Their opinion can't change your value. Just because they "appraised" you at a lower worth doesn't change the truth that Jesus spilled His blood and paid the highest price to purchase your freedom.

I hear it said so often by Christians that "we're so unworthy!" While I understand the sentiment, God does not share that opinion of you. In and of yourself, your performance does NOT make you worthy. But His precious blood DID make you worthy. No, you don't deserve it and you can't earn it, but Jesus bought your redemption with His life. *He* made you worthy! You didn't buy yourself, so you can't set your own value.

I've heard other Christians say something along the lines of "God, here's my heart. It's not much but here it is." Again, I understand the sentiment, but think about how insulting that must be to Jesus. He went through all He did, bearing the weight of our sins, atoning for them with His blood, sacrificing His life so we could be reconciled back unto God. Jesus was sent here by God for the sole purpose of redeeming you and cleansing your heart. I'd say He values the gift of your heart quite a bit.

Knowing how much you mean to God allows you to live a life free from insecurity. Boldness, confidence, and security all require a source, they come from knowing something. Let me give you an example.

Since you're taking the time to read my book, allow me to tell you a little bit about myself. I was born and raised in Athens, GA, and I'm the third born of four kids. I've been a pastor's kid for as long as I can remember, and I'm an avid Georgia Bulldogs fan.[5] I've trained in martial arts, enjoy action movies, and love my amazingly beautiful wife more than anything. In addition to all this, anyone who knows me well knows I also really love Cheez-Itz! They are hands down my #1 snack of choice.

---

[5] Note from the editor: Go Dawgs!

81

To this day, whenever I go to my parent's house, I always open the pantry and search for a box of Cheez-Itz. I'm so confident in my parents' love for me that I, with full confidence of faith, just walk in and take their hard-earned Cheez-Itz. Now, I don't take the snack because I paid for it or earned it, quite the contrary I didn't even pick them up from the store. However, I still have every bit of boldness to claim my snack because I am confident in my relationship with my parents and their love for me as their son.

But let's say you invited me to your house. I would not approach your pantry with the same level of confidence and boldness because there's not the same certainty in our relationship as in my relationship with my parents. Relationship changes everything.

The level of confidence, boldness, and security you possess in this life is directly connected to what you believe about your relationship with God.

As a son or daughter of Almighty God, you were placed on this earth for a purpose. God does not make mistakes, and you are no accident. You were put here as an ambassador for Christ Jesus. He became your substitute and took on all your sin and shame. He first identified with us in our mess so we can now identify with Him in His victory.

Jesus has made us Kings and priests, created to rule and reign in this life. (Revelation 5:10) You were never meant to live in bondage as a slave to the devil and his plans. On the contrary, God gave you a place of authority over the enemy, and the same power that raised Jesus from the dead is alive and dwells inside of you.

It's the enemy's strategy to force you back under his oppression by deceiving you into adopting insecurity and shame. But the good news is, my friend, Jesus defeated all of hell through His death, burial, and resurrection. And His victory is our victory! Praise God!

Check out this scripture from the book of Colossians:

"Then Jesus made a public spectacle of all the powers and principalities of darkness, stripping away from them every weapon and all their spiritual authority and power to accuse us, and by the power of the cross, Jesus led them around as prisoners in a procession of triumph. He was not their prisoner; they were His."

Colossians 2:15 TPT

You are not a slave to sin or the devil. You're not destined for defeat and failure. Jesus went to battle on your behalf and won the victory. The only authority the devil had over humanity was sin, and Jesus eradicated that. There is no more sin stain on our account. His blood cleansed us and made us brand new!

So now, the devil will try and use shame and condemnation to get you to fall back into the trap of insecurity. He'll bring up things from your past, reminding you of all the times you missed it. His goal is to convince you of the lie that you're still "just an old sinner," and thereby get you to surrender the power and authority you have been given in Christ. The enemy will constantly be in your ear, condemning you as a nobody who can't seem to get control of the flesh.

Let me tell you, you're not alone in this. The devil uses and has used this same tired tactic for thousands of years. He even used it on the Apostle Paul. Let's look at what Paul had to say about the devil's schemes in the book of Romans:

"My lofty desires to do what is good are dashed when I do the things I want to avoid. So, if my behavior contradicts my desires to do good, I must conclude that it's not my true identity doing it, but the unwelcome intruder of sin hindering me from being who I really am. Through my experience of this principle, I discover that even when I want to do good, evil is ready to sabotage me. Truly, deeply within my true identity, I love to do what pleases God. But I discern another power operating in my humanity, waging a war against the moral principles of my conscience and bringing me into captivity as a prisoner to the "law" of sin - this unwelcome intruder in my humanity. What an agonizing situation I am in! So, who has the power to rescue this miserable man from the unwelcome intruder of sin and death? I give all my thanks to God, for His mighty power has finally provided a way out through our Lord Jesus, the Anointed One! So if left to myself, the flesh aligns with the law of sin, but now my renewed mind is fixed on and submitted to God's righteous principles."

Romans 7:19-25 TPT

What the enemy loves to do is tempt you with sin, tell you that the sin is good for you. Then if you yield to that temptation and sin, he immediately comes and beats you over the head with shame, guilt, and condemnation. That seems to be a cycle so many find themselves in, almost like an endless loop. The end result is usually acceptance of the lie that your mistakes have separated you from God—a breeding ground of insecurity. But Praise God forever, there is freedom readily available for us! There is a way of escaping the cycle.

"But Pastor Jonathan," you may say, "I'm still yielding to sin. I'm still yielding to temptation from the devil."

That's why Romans 8:1 was written. It says, *"There is therefore now no condemnation to those who are in Christ."* Breaking free from the chains of guilt, shame, and condemnation is what breaks that ugly cycle of sin in our lives.

Friend, God wants you to live in a realm of life and freedom, away from the oppression and bondage of the enemy. The Holy Spirit, through the Apostle Paul, put it like this:

*"This 'realm of death' describes our **former** state, for we were held in sin's grasp. But now we've been resurrected out of that 'realm of death' **never to return,** for we are forever alive and forgiven of all our sins."*

Colossians 2:13 TPT (Emphasis mine)

Our justification in Christ has broken sin's former power over us! We are no longer slaves to the enemy but have become children of God. We've been set free! You don't have to be afraid of the power of sin coming back to haunt you again. Jesus obtained that victory for you, and what He provides, He will maintain. Simply believe in Him, believe that you are who He says you are. You'll find a new sense of confidence and security as you've never experienced before, and no devil in hell nor person on the earth can ever rob you of it.

The Apostle Paul had this same revelation of his new identity in Christ, and it gave him boldness and provided security throughout his tumultuous life. He had this to say to the Church at Philippi:

"For we are the circumcision, who worship God in the Spirit, rejoice in Christ Jesus, and have no confidence in the flesh, though I also might have confidence in the flesh. If anyone else thinks he may have confidence in the flesh, I more so: circumcised the eighth day, of the stock of Israel, of the tribe of Benjamin, a Hebrew of the Hebrews; concerning the law, a Pharisee; concerning zeal, persecuting the church; concerning the righteousness which is in the law, blameless. But what things were gain to me, these I have counted loss for Christ. Yet indeed I also count all things loss for the excellence of the knowledge of Christ Jesus my Lord, for whom I have suffered the loss of all things, and count them as rubbish, that I may gain Christ and be found in Him, not having my own righteousness, which is from

the law, but that which is through faith in Christ, the
righteousness which is from God by faith"

Philippians 3:3-9

If anyone had a reason to trust in their flesh, it was the
Apostle Paul, yet even he considered his own self-
righteousness inferior and worthless compared to the
gift he (just like us) had access to in Christ. He mentions
the family he came from, his knowledge and degrees as
a teacher of the law, and even how zealous and
passionate he was for his religion (even if it was
misplaced). All of these things could be considered, by
the world's standards, a good foundation for security.
There's just one problem, all of these things are
temporary. They can be brought to nothing in but a
moment. They create nothing more than a false sense
of security.

Uncertainty in your identity can easily give way to
insecurity. So, the devil will exploit any crack or weak
spot in your identity, to weigh you down. If I went to
this school, then I'd be ok. If I went to this church, then
I'd be ok. If I had this job, then I'd be ok. If I married that
person, then I'd be ok. If I had this amount of money,
then I'd be ok. If I was better connected, then I'd be ok.
If my political party is in office, then I'd be ok. These
things may provide momentary relief, but they're all
incredibly fragile. These things are simply incapable of
sustaining you through the ups and downs of this life.

Paul saw who he was in Christ and chose to derive his
worth from there. Nothing else could give him that

same level of confidence as the revelation of what he had in Jesus. That's why he never looked for anyone else's approval.

There's a popular TV show called The Voice. Each season it shows thousands of hopeful contestants who will sing to show they have what it takes to make it in the music industry. The best part of the show to me is always the auditions. You have people from all walks of life who come to showcase their skills and hopefully get at least one judge to notice and affirm their talent. The judges begin with their backs to the contestants at the start of the performance. If a judge likes what they hear, they'll turn around to show their approval of the contestant's voice. Some make it, many don't.

But the interesting part to me is that we do the same thing every day at this stage of life, whether we realize it or not. We put people in the judges' seat, people whose acceptance and approval we yearn for. We will spend weeks and months trying everything we can to get them to turn their chair and notice us. To get them to add us to their "team." The kicker of it all? Most of the time these "judges" we're trying so hard to impress don't even have a clue that we're looking to them. They don't even know they're supposed to turn around and notice us. People can spend years disappointed that they didn't get the approval they hoped for when all the while the so-called "judges" didn't even realize the "show" was happening... The people we try to impress really couldn't care less.

Why are we doing that? Because we haven't yet established our hearts in the identity given to us by our Heavenly Father. We're trying to gain other people's approval because we don't know that we have His. We're seeking validation from other people rather than from God.

Here's where your whole life can change! When you fully know how loved you are and that you already have the acceptance and approval of God, Planet Creator, the Most High, the King of Kings and Lord of Lords, the very One whose name causes demons to tremble. When you know you have His approval, why would you ever seek the approval of anyone else? Why would I ever compromise or waste time feeling disappointed because someone didn't notice me when Almighty God has my picture on His fridge? My friend, this is true freedom and security!

Of course, we all want to be liked, we all want to feel accepted, and we all want a close community of friends. These desires are from the Lord Himself. But let me share some liberating truths with you- not everyone is going to like you. Not everyone is going to accept you. Not everyone is going to turn their chair and notice you. But Jesus already has. He turned His chair for you 2000 years ago when He hung on a cross as an open and public display of love for you. He hung on that cross to prove to you that you have His approval. He made a spot on His team specifically for you.

When I receive this truth from my gracious Heavenly Father, I won't need anything from anyone else. I'll truly be in a place where I can love others the way He has loved me.

Accepting God's love for us shifts our focus so that we live for Jesus and Jesus alone. This is what allows you to truly put your heart into all you do. You'll become such a person of excellence. We'll find that our heart's desire is to bring honor and glory to Jesus in all we say and do because we're doing it for Him, and not for anyone else. More than anything, this kind of belief takes me out of the center of my life. I no longer need to get something out of everyone around me but can instead love and minister to them. When Jesus takes His place at the center of my life, He'll see to it that I'm in the right place at the right time doing the right thing with the right people—all the time.

This way of living takes a tremendous amount of pressure off of my relationships. It stops me from looking to people who are not Jesus to try and be Jesus for me. I'll stop looking to my spouse to give me security. I'll stop looking to my friends to constantly validate my worth and value. This will help free me from anger, bitterness, and offense in all of my relationships.

My dear friend, holding onto offense and bitterness is a choice. You can choose to let that go today. I'm not here to justify the mean and hurtful things someone else may have said or done to you. I don't want to belittle the pain. You may have every right to hold unforgiveness and bitterness towards them. People are people and they won't always get it right. Even those who are close to you and truly do love and care for you will mess up and hurt you from time to time. We are all susceptible to making mistakes, and we all need grace and mercy. But staying bitter will hinder you from living and walking in all God has for you.

Because we know who we are in Christ and we know how much He's forgiven us, we can be quick to forgive and quick to let go of bitterness and offense. When an opportunity to become bitter arises, we can run to Jesus and be reminded of His love for us. He can minister healing to you and restore you back to your rightful place as a child of God.

If you're a pastor or a minister, can I talk to you for a minute? Don't ever allow your security or your identity to be rooted in your ministry. Your calling is important. Following Jesus and proclaiming His Word is vital. But if you preach a message to get praise and validation from people, you'll live your life on a roller coaster of emotions. Go back to your first love, Jesus. Find your identity in Him, not how many people you preach to on any given Sunday. Find your security in Him, not in how many "amens" you get during a sermon.

The Lord said this to me a couple of years ago: "You always minister *to* people, but you minister *for* me." What a difference that has made for my life and ministry! I don't have to come up with some entertaining sermon that will provoke a certain response. If I find myself doing that, then my purpose is no longer to get something to anyone but rather to get something from people. For a minister of the Gospel, this should never be. But thank God, we can stand confident in who we are in Jesus, minister words of life to people, and see their lives transformed by the Spirit of God. That's what it's all about anyway.

Security is a matter of the heart. It's a matter of how I see myself. It's a matter of who is at the center of my life. This is what true security looks like: an individual rooted and grounded in their identity in Christ.

Chapter 7: Change of Clothes

When I was a teenager in the youth group at my church, we took a trip down to a popular mall outside of Atlanta. There was a guy in our group who wasn't exactly known for his fashion sense. He showed up wearing camouflage cargo shorts, black cowboy boots, a bright orange jersey, and a black cowboy hat. It was almost as if he picked all of his favorite articles of clothing and just put them together with no fashion sense whatsoever. The burning question we all had for him was simply, "why?" That question remains unanswered for me even to this day.

The big kicker is I wish I could say that only happened once, but it did not. It happened so often that the only logical conclusion was that—somehow—he must have really believed he looked great. The thought I kept having was "Is that really what you decided to wear? I've seen you wear other things, yet somehow this outfit is what you went with? On purpose?"

I'm not here to rag on other people's wardrobe choices. I know I've also worn outfits in the past that should have never been seen in public. But I've noticed something in following Jesus, just like there are certain outfits I should rid my closet of naturally, there are some spiritual "clothes" that should be tossed out too. Just like my friend's horrendous fashion choices in the natural realm, those spiritual "clothes" are out of style.

They're raggedy, they're old, and, frankly, you've just outgrown them.

Think about how ridiculous and uncomfortable it would be for you to continue wearing the same clothes you were when you were five years old. That'd be ridiculous! Because of the massive amount of physical change that (hopefully) took place between now and then, it is impossible for you to go back to wearing those old clothes. Likewise, after the massive change that took place in your spirit when you received your new identity in Jesus, those old "clothes" attached to your old identity just don't fit you anymore.

Throughout this chapter, we're going to look at some scriptures that show us why we needed a change of spiritual clothes and what kind of new threads we now have access to in Jesus.

First, let's talk about where our clothes come from. Spiritually speaking, we no longer need to provide our own garments. It's when we forget who we are and what we have in Christ that we start trying to clothe and cover ourselves.

We've talked about Genesis 3 and when Adam and Eve ate the forbidden fruit throughout some of our previous chapters. We have touched on how the serpent deceived them into thinking their identity was incomplete. He said to them "in the day you eat of it [the forbidden fruit] your eyes will be opened, and you will be like God, knowing good and evil." Sadly, they of course ate the fruit and they saw that they were naked. Interestingly, the very first thing they did was sew fig leaves together to make coverings for themselves.

Is that not a pretty accurate depiction of most of us? We try to solve a permanent problem with a temporary solution. The fig leaves Adam and Eve sewed together would wither away, rather quickly I might add, and then what? They'd spend most of their days attempting to cover themselves over and over with things that simply fade and wither away. And I'd venture to say that even when they had their fig leaf outfits on, they still felt exposed. Similarly for us, no matter how hard we try or how long we try, we are never able to truly cover ourselves. Despite our best efforts, we still end up feeling exposed, unprotected, and uncomfortable.

That's why I love what God did for mankind in Genesis 3:21. It says, "And the Lord God made clothing from animal skins for Adam and his wife." At that moment, God was showing unmerited love and grace toward His creations. God had every right to leave them in their withering fig leaves, but instead, He chose to provide them with a proper covering that would last far longer...

This is the first ever animal sacrifice recorded in Scripture and doubles as a beautiful picture of the Lord Jesus... He is the true sacrificial gift, straight from God Himself, that covers us and every trace of our sins. We no longer have to feel exposed to our shame. What a wonderful God He is!

Sin always tries to make us feel exposed, to put the focus on our own inability to cover ourselves. Grace always comes to put the focus on the blood of Jesus and its ability to cover us. He's got you covered. Galatians 3:27, TPT says *"Faith immersed you into Christ, and now you are covered and clothed with His life."*

Remember the parable of the Prodigal Son in Luke 15? The Prodigal Son did nothing but live recklessly and dishonor his father. His goal was to feed his own ego and pleasure his own flesh. When he ran out of money, was stuck taking care of pigs, and finally came to the end of himself, he remembered the provision of his father's house and began his journey home. In his mind, he was content to return as a meager servant, not a son. He thought his past mistakes disqualified him from his place of sonship. He spent his whole trip home writing a speech for his father, groveling for forgiveness and begging to return as a lowly farmhand. But things went quite differently. When the Prodigal Son came into view of his father's house, the father saw him coming and came sprinting up the road to meet him. Rather than reprimand the boy, His father hugged and kissed him, welcoming him back with open arms. In that moment, the son tried to launch into his speech of unworthiness. But before he could even finish the first few lines, his father interrupted him. Turning to his servants, the father exclaimed: *"Quick, bring me the **best** robe, **my very own robe**, and I will place it on his shoulders. Bring the ring, the seal of sonship, and I will* *put it on his finger. And bring the best shoes you can find for my son."* Luke 15:22 TPT (Emphasis mine)

Look at the gracious response of the father. He stopped the Prodigal Son mid-speech to restore him back to his full position in the family. I'm sure the son's clothes were stinky, raggedy, and stained from his time taking care of pigs. His father saw those rags and said, "This won't do!" But he didn't just ask one of his servants for one of their robes. He said "Go get the *best* robe. Go get *my very own* robe." Imagine what that spoke to the son. Having done nothing to earn it, he has been given his father's robe, the best and most expensive robe available.

My friend, this is exactly what your Heavenly Father did for you. The Lord saw the clothes we had been wearing from the world. Clothes that smelled, were raggedy and had been stained from the curse of sin. God said, "Nope, this just won't do!" So, He gave us the best robe, He gave us His robe! A robe made for someone in the royal family.

Isaiah 61:10 says that God has "clothed us with the garments of salvation, and covered us in a robe of righteousness." When we accepted Jesus, we traded in the old rags of who we used to be and received a new royal robe of righteousness, God's *very own* robe of righteousness.

Regardless of how we feel or whether we think we deserve it or not, we need to take that robe, put it on, look in the mirror and say, "This fits me perfectly!" Your New Creation identity in Christ fits in your Father's robe perfectly.

Don't choose to go back to your old clothes just because you feel like you don't deserve your Father's new threads. The Bible says that our self-righteousness is as filthy rags[6]. That means our works will never be enough to cover us and make us clean. That's why we needed Jesus. We needed a Spotless Lamb to take our place and be what we couldn't be. His precious blood brought us from rags to righteousness.

I like to call them "church clothes." If you grew up going to church, do you remember those outfits your parents forced you to wear for service? Maybe your family referred to it as your "Sunday best."

When I was a kid, I hated wearing "church clothes"! I never really liked feeling confined in a suit with a tie, especially during the hot summer months in the deep south. So, when I was about 7 or 8 years old, I got A bright idea on how to get out of wearing the uncomfortable outfits I so disdained. I would run up and down the front of our church and slide across the carpet on my knees. In no time at all I would tear holes in the knees of my dress pants. Boy, my mom would get so upset with me! The following week, she would take me shopping and get me a new pair of pants for church.

---

[6] If you aren't easily offended, check out "filthy rags" in the original Greek. It gets the point across a little better.

Come Sunday morning right after service, I'd start running and sliding again, tearing holes in the knees of my new pants. So, my mom would discipline me, try to get me to stop, and then before the next Sunday, she'd get me another pair of pants.

It seemed like the ultimate chess match between my mom and me. I will say, now that I've grown, I see the value in not ruining my clothes every week. I don't think my wife would appreciate it if I continued that behavior today.

While our outward church clothes may have changed in style and appearance over the last several decades (thank the Lord), the "spiritual clothes" we've been given as New Creations in Christ are perfect and eternal. And these spiritual threads aren't just for Sunday—we should be wearing them every single day.

Ephesians chapter 4 says *"If indeed you have heard Him and have been taught by Him, as the truth is in Jesus: that **you put off**, concerning your former conduct, the old man which grows corrupt according to the deceitful lusts, and be renewed in the spirit of your mind, and that **you put on** the new man which was created according to God, in true righteousness and holiness."*

Ephesians 4:21-24 (Emphasis Mine)

Some of us remember to put on our new spiritual clothes when we go to church on Sunday, but neglect to wear them through the rest of our week. We forget them while at work, at school, at home, or at the store.

We constantly change our wardrobe based on the location or situation we're in. We try to blend into our environment rather than influence and change the world around us through the Holy Spirit.

I love the imagery in these scriptures! We are meant to have a change of clothes when we receive Jesus. Instead of wearing depression, we can put on joy. Rather than wearing anxiety and worry, we can change into the robes of peace and composure.

This concept of putting off something old in exchange for something new is a common theme throughout Scripture.

Isaiah 61 tells us to put on "the garments of praise for the spirit of heaviness." Something I have noticed during my walk with the Lord and my time in ministry is that far too many children of God choose to walk through this life heavy and weighed down. They haven't changed their clothes yet. They're still walking around with the old rags associated with the "old man" mentioned in Ephesians.

It is not God's will for you to walk through this life burdened down and depressed. Jesus said *"Come to Me, all you who labor and are heavy laden, and I will give you rest. Take My yoke upon you and learn from Me, for I am gentle and lowly in heart, and you will find rest for your souls. For My yoke is **easy** and My burden is **light**."* Matthew 11:28-30 (Emphasis mine)

I love how simple Jesus makes it for us to understand. If I may reverently paraphrase for a moment, Jesus is essentially saying, "If it's easy, it's from Me. If it's heavy, it's not Me." God doesn't intend for you to live your life on the struggle bus, never really going anywhere. He has made you in His likeness and image. That means you were imagined in the very mind of God, and He created you to do great things—to conquer! The reason we start feeling heavy is that we put on the cares of our own life, an outfit we were never designed to bear.

To put this another way, living with burden and care is to live as if our lives were our own responsibility. And if you believe your life is your own *responsibility*, then you must constantly *respond* with your own *ability*. But God, your Heavenly Father, sees you as His responsibility. When you trust Him and cast your care over on Him, He can and will respond with His ability. He not only wants you to have life but also to enjoy it to the fullest (John 10:10). A major deciding factor in whether you enjoy the life God has graciously made available to you is what you decide to put off and what you decide to put on.

When you throw off those clothes of heaviness and put on the garment of praise, that's when you start enjoying the life Jesus died to give you. Even when you're going through a storm, you can have peace. Listen, the truth is that in this life you will face trials, and you will go through sticky situations and turbulent circumstances. But you can either go through them with peace and joy, singing praise and magnifying God, or you can go through trials full of stress, worry, and depression, only opening your mouth to magnify the problem.

Even now, before you see any change on the outside when everything still appears to be the same in the natural, you can lift your voice and begin praising and thanking God for His goodness and His precious promises. Once you've received Christ, don't leave those new clothes in your closet. Throw off your old rags and enjoy your new threads.

Let's think back for a moment to my old friend from youth group who would wear questionable outfits. I'm sure his mom asked him "Is that what you're going to wear? Is that really what you want to wear out?" In hopes of stirring his thought process and prompting him to change his outfit. Similarly, for us today, when we go back to our old spiritual clothes, those rags of self-focused and performance-based living, God's Spirit on the inside asks "Is that what you're going to wear? Is that really what you want to wear out?" Let's not follow the example of my old friend and be stubborn to the point of looking criminally unfashionable. There is no comparison between what we used to have and what the Lord has made available to us. The clothes of the old man will never compare to the clothes of the new man in Christ.

All of us have that one shirt or that pair of pants that just sits in our closet. We never wear it for fear of ruining it. I know I've certainly done this sort of thing before. I'll get a shirt and wear it once and it becomes my favorite shirt, but then I hang it up and leave it in my closet. I can't explain why I do that, but I do. Maybe I feel like it'll fade, or I'll mess it up. However, I can assure you that these new clothes given to you by God Himself will never fade, never shrink, and never get dirty. Try as you might, you will never be able to mess them up. These supernatural clothes are meant to be worn eternally—but they can't be worn out.

My friend, today is a new day for you. You can put on these new clothes. It reminds me of those 1980s John Hughes movies. You'd have an unsuspecting person who gets this radical makeover and reveals this suave, cool, collected person. When Jesus became your Lord and Savior, He gave you a complete transformation on the inside. And now you've got something on the inside constantly working to align your outside with what God says about you.

Think about it, clothes even have the power to define parts of who you are as a person. They can reveal the company you work for, your favorite sports team, what colors you like and dislike, and places you've visited around the world. We have clothes for just about every occasion in life: church, weddings, work, travel, fitness, cold weather, hot weather—you name it. Our clothes can also be a powerful indicator of where we're going and what we're planning to do when we get there. In some ways the old saying is true, clothes really do make the man.

The story of Blind Bartimaeus from Mark chapter 10 fits right in with what we're talking about here. As Jesus was leaving the city of Jericho, Bartimaeus sat begging on the roadside where Jesus was walking.
When Bartimaeus heard it was Jesus passing by, he cried out to Jesus asking Him to have mercy on him. Some of Jesus' followers tried to shut Blind Bartimaeus up, but the beggar cried out all the more. Then, a miracle happens. The Son of God, the Savior of the world, *"stood still and commanded him to be called"* (Mark 10:49). God Himself stopped in His tracks to minister to a lowly beggar. Then comes verse 50, which is where I want to focus. It says, *"And throwing aside his garment, he [Bartimaeus] rose and came to Jesus"* (Mark 10:50, brackets mine).

According to historical context, Bartimaeus's garment very likely would have been a cloak issued by the local government to verify that he was legitimately blind. As weird as it sounds, it almost functioned like a license to beg and collect alms. In essence, this cloak represented his state-sanctioned right to beg. Bartimaeus' cloak is what identified him as a disabled beggar. Clearly, this cloak would have been very valuable to him and would have provided a sense of safety and security for him.

But look at the level of expectancy Bartimaeus had when Jesus called him! He threw off his garment. This is a key point here; the cloak didn't just happen to fall off.

104

He made a choice to put off what represented his old identity as a beggar because he knew that, after a few moments with Jesus, he wouldn't need that ever again.

Maybe you find yourself with your own "cloak" that identifies you. Maybe a friend, a parent, a diagnosis, or even the government has given you garments to identify you. Let me encourage you to do just what Bartimaeus did—throw off those man-made identities and run to Jesus. He is calling you by name. By faith, you can stand up with a heart full of expectancy and cast aside those garments of heaviness, put off those clothes of the curse, and throw away those threads of the past. Instead, put on the clothes of who you are now in Jesus: the new man, forever under the blessing. And just like the Prodigal Son's father gave him a new robe to identify what family he belonged to; your Heavenly Father has given you the righteous robes of your new family—the family of God.

Chapter 8: Victor Not Victim

As I mentioned earlier, I am an avid fan of the University of Georgia football program. Even as a little boy, I loved watching the Bulldogs with my family on Saturday afternoons. Every year, we would start with such hope and excitement at the possibility of winning the National Championship and victoriously hoisting the championship trophy. For many years, that didn't quite work out. Some years we came to the brink of victory just to throw it all away at the last second. After a forty-year championship drought, many people had given up hope of the Dawgs ever winning another title. That is, of course, until the night of January 10, 2022. I won't soon forget that day. It was the day The Georgia Bulldogs football team stopped being victims and became victors—they became champions.

I remember watching the game with some friends and feeling a sense of very cautious optimism. After being burned as many times as we had, University of Georgia fans have a hard time embracing hope. Iconic images of past postseason failures were prevalent in my mind for most of the game. Until, with just over a minute left in the fourth quarter, everything changed. A Georgia defender made the play of his life. Leaping into the air, he intercepted a pass and ran it back almost 80 yards for a touchdown. In one play, we had cemented the victory! Let me tell you, my friends and I went wild![7] We were screaming, jumping, and carrying on for quite some time. After 40 years of heartbreak, the team we'd cheered on for decades had finally become victors! It was a great day for us and for the entire city.

Since that great day in January, I've gone back several times to rewatch the game. However, now when I watch it, there's a big difference in my perspective. No matter how many times we drop a pass or don't score, I'm not nervous about the outcome. I'm not nervous because I know something now that I didn't know when the game was being played. I know the final score. I *know* we end up as champions, so I even view the mistakes we made through a lens of victory.

There's a strong parallel here to what we can experience as children of the Almighty God! We have the ability to look at our life through the lens of victory.

In Romans 8, the Holy Spirit through the Apostle Paul produces some of the most powerful words ever recorded in scripture. Take a look:

"What then shall we say to these things? If God is for us, who can be against us? He who did not spare His own Son, but delivered Him up for us all, how shall He not with Him also freely give us all things?

---

[7] The editor of this book was on campus for the game and fell off a giant stone column in the ensuing madness. Worth it.

Who shall bring a charge against God's elect? It is God who justifies. Who is he who condemns? It is Christ who died, and furthermore is also risen, who is even at the right hand of God, who also makes intercession for us. Who shall separate us from the love of Christ? Shall tribulation, or distress, or persecution, or famine, or nakedness, or peril, or sword? As it is written:

> *"For Your sake we are killed all day long; We are accounted as sheep for the slaughter."*

*Yet in all these things **we are more than conquerors through Him** who loved us. For I am persuaded that neither death nor life, nor angels nor principalities nor powers, nor things present nor things to come, nor height nor depth, nor any other created thing, shall be able to separate us from the love of God which is in Christ Jesus our Lord."*

Romans 8:31-39 (Emphasis mine)

There are two major themes in this passage of scripture. The first is the unconditional, everlasting love of God for us. There is nothing and no one who could ever separate us from the love Our Heavenly Father has for us. His love is so great and so vast and so strong that nothing can ever separate us from it, nor cause it to wither or fade away. Always remember this, even when the enemy, the accuser of your soul, tells you that you've done too much wrong, you've wandered too far off, or that you've made yourself unlovable and unreachable by your Heavenly Father. My friend, the devil is a liar. Satan will constantly lie to you about your position in Christ and the love Jesus has for you because he is terrified of the day you discover the truth—the day you discover the rich inheritance you have in Christ. This brings us to our second theme, that *"we are more than conquerors through Him who loved us."*

I love how verse 37 begins. It starts with these words, *"Yet in all these things…"* In the middle of the trial, in the face of the obstacle, when the devil deals his hardest blow your way, that is when you stand as more than a conqueror through "Him" (Jesus).

Now, don't forget, the most important part of that verse is the *why*. Why are we more than conquerors? It's not because of our own effort. It's not because of our performance. It's certainly not because we deserve it. On the contrary, it's solely dependent on Jesus and His love for us. Because Jesus beat death, hell, and the grave, so have we. Our identity is wrapped in and joined together with His. Jesus' victory is our victory.

Today, you can start seeing yourself as a victor in life and not a victim of life. Life's circumstances and challenges happen to everyone, but we have a choice in how we see and respond to them. The enemy loves to try and get us to identify with our current circumstances, to force us into the trap of victim-mentality. The devil wants us to believe that we are completely powerless in this life and that the best we can do is cope with the hardships that come our way. My friend, nothing could be further from the truth.

As the Body of Christ, we were never meant to cope, we were meant to conquer. We aren't supposed to find a way to manage the mountain, we're supposed to speak to the mountain and command it to be removed. God doesn't desire for us to live in struggle, He desires for us to live in success. We don't have to be in crisis, we are in Christ.

Jesus said, *"Whatever you bind on earth is bound in Heaven, and whatever you loose on earth is loosed in Heaven."* (Matthew 18:18) The same Spirit, the same life, and the same power that raised Jesus up from the dead is alive and dwells on the inside of you. It sounds to me that being a victim was never a part of God's plan for you. His plan was for us, His children, to rule and reign on the earth. Let me show you:

*"Death once held us in its grip, and by the blunder of one man, death reigned as king over humanity. But now, how much more are we held in the grip of grace and continue **reigning as kings in life** enjoying our regal freedom through the gift of perfect righteousness in the One and Only Jesus, the Messiah!"* Romans 5:17 TPT (Emphasis Mine)

*"The Heavens belong to our God; they are His alone, but He has given us the earth and **put us in charge**."* Psalm 115:16 TPT (Emphasis Mine)

*"You have delegated to them rulership over all You have made, with **everything under their authority** placing earth itself under the feet of your image-bearers."* Psalm 8:6 TPT (Emphasis Mine)

These three scriptures, along with many others that I could list, emphatically declare God's will for us to rule with the authority He gave to us. This concept was so important to God that He made it a part of the very first command given to Adam and Eve in the Garden:

*Then God said, "Let Us make man in Our image, according to Our likeness; **let them have dominion** over the fish of the sea, over the birds of the air, and over the cattle, over all the earth and over every creeping thing that creeps on the earth." So God created man in His own image; in the image of God He created him; male and female He created them. Then God blessed them, and God said to them, "Be fruitful and multiply; fill the earth and subdue it; **have dominion** over the fish of the sea, over the birds of the air, and over every living thing that moves on the earth."*

Genesis 1:26-28 (Emphasis Mine)

This is God's original intent for man. The Lord designed *us* to be in command on this Earth, not the enemy. Look at God's instructions in verse 28, He said, *"have dominion over the birds of the air, over the fish of the sea, and every living thing that moves on the earth."* God basically said, "If it moves, it's subject to you."

This conversation between God and man would prove to be extremely consequential in the following chapters. Adam and Eve *should* have used their authority and dominion to command the serpent to leave the garden when he slithered with his subtle temptation. This is what I believe God was endeavoring to prepare them for when He gave them command. They sure could have saved us all a lot of time and hassle by properly using their God-given authority.

Flash forward to the New Testament, and this is how we see Jesus operating here on Earth. We see Him commanding sickness to leave. We see Him command the storm to be still. We see Him command the dead to be raised. Even while He preached and prayed, those around Him took notice of His boldness. They quite literally said, *"He was teaching them as one having authority, and not as the scribes"* (Mark 1:22). I remember a few years ago, some of my co-workers asked me to pray for a mutual friend who was diagnosed with cancer. I always jump at the opportunity to curse the enemy's works and speak life over people. It brings me great joy to make the devil mad. So, we all gathered one morning and I began to pray. I cursed that cancer in Jesus' Name, commanded it to leave the person's body, and spoke the Healing power of God into the situation to bring healing and wholeness. When I finished praying, I looked up and a few of my coworkers were staring at me in surprise. One gentleman spoke up and said, "I haven't ever heard anyone pray like that before!" I'm guessing he was used to the frothy "if it be

Thy will, Lord" religious kind of prayers. Not someone who stood bold, confident, and with full assurance of faith—*knowing* the will of God. After all, the will of God is the Word of God. We can pray bold, confident prayers knowing we won't fall because we have the firm foundation of God's Word beneath our feet.

Believe it or not, whenever Jesus encountered a person oppressed with sickness, He rarely prayed for healing in the traditional religious sense. Instead, He spoke to the disease, and it obeyed. One story in particular that has always encouraged me is found in the Gospel of Luke.

*"Now He was teaching in one of the synagogues on the Sabbath. And behold, there was a woman who had a spirit of infirmity eighteen years, and was bent over and could in no way raise herself up. But when Jesus saw her, He called her to Him and said to her, "**Woman, you are loosed from your infirmity.**" And He laid His hands on her, and immediately she was made straight, and glorified God.*

But the ruler of the synagogue answered with indignation, because Jesus had healed on the Sabbath; and he said to the crowd, "There are six days on which men ought to work; therefore come and be healed on them, and not on the Sabbath day."

The Lord then answered him and said, "Hypocrite! Does not each one of you on the Sabbath loose his ox or donkey from the stall, and lead it away to water it? So ought not this woman, being a daughter of Abraham, whom Satan has bound—think of it—for eighteen years, be loosed from this bond on the Sabbath?" Luke 13:10-16 (emphasis mine).

Through His ministry, Jesus would use the concept of identity to free people from the oppression of the enemy. When Jesus witnessed this woman's affliction, He stopped and told her who she really was, a *free* daughter of God. Details are very important in the Bible, and Jesus never minces words. He deliberately declared to the woman *"you are loosed."* The verb here denotes a state of existing, a state of identity. Jesus didn't say "go work to get loosed," but instead He spoke a new identity over the woman, the way God saw her as a beloved daughter of Abraham. And this isn't an isolated incident. We see Jesus employing this kind of language throughout the New Testament. He repeatedly told people who they were, rather than what they had to do, as a means to free them from oppression.

The devil works with identity too, doing his best to deceive us right into bondage. Sadly, this is happening to millions of people every single day. If we are deceived into believing his lies about our identity, he can keep us living in bondage rather than experiencing the abundant life God intends for us to live.

Here are some of the common lies I've seen people believe and have even temporarily fallen for myself:

- Being sick is a normal part of life.
- I'm on a fixed, limited income.

- I'm young, I have to wait to be used by God.
- I'm old, it's too late for me to be used by God.
- I lose strength, energy, and health as I age.
- God won't help me as long as I'm in sin.
- All young people have to be broke and deeply in debt.

These, among so many other lies, are poisoning the minds of people all over the world. Some have been circulated and passed down for generations, others for millennia. Oftentimes, we believe these lies because either we don't know God has qualified us for more or because we feel like we don't deserve more. In our minds, we assume that we could never deserve the abundant goodness of God because we could never qualify for it ourselves. The second part of that statement is actually true, and, amazingly, that very fact is what qualifies us for help in the first place. Our complete inability to save ourselves is what qualifies us for the superabundant grace of God. And once this revelation of God's grace progresses beyond being something we've just heard about and becomes something we believe in our hearts, we'll finally have the courage to walk it out.

Boldness has to have a source. To be bold, you need to know something. That's why getting in the Word of God every day is so vital for our growth and success in life. One minister said it like this, "Faith begins where the will of God is known." That's so true! When you know what God's will is for you in an area, you can launch out in faith and take hold of that promise with full expectation of it manifesting in your life. Determining God's will on a subject is not hard. He gave us His Word, the Bible, which lays out in detail His exact will for you in every area of life. You can know the will of God for your life, and when you know it, you can be bold about living in it.

Understanding God's will and our new identity in Christ all ties back into the topic of God-given authority that we discussed earlier. Once we know these two key factors, we can properly operate in our authority. Don't let the enemy undermine your faith with doubt and unbelief. Stand bold! Stand confident! Don't lose heart! If you'll continue to believe His Word, you will see the goodness of God show up in your life. Why is it so important for us as children of God to take our place and rule with the authority given to us in Christ? Because if we don't rule and reign, the enemy will. Authority on this Earth is like a vacuum, and something is going to fill it. That's why the devil fights so hard to deceive you and thereby keep you under his thumb. Jesus defeated hell at the cross, but if we keep quiet and stay hidden, then there'll be no one to enforce the defeat.

I heard one Pastor say it this way, "When you reign, addiction doesn't. When you reign, fear doesn't. When you reign, sickness doesn't. When you reign, the enemy doesn't." I'm not saying that we are Jesus, but I am saying He gave us His authority. Scripture clearly tells us that we have the same power of God and position with God that Jesus has. 1 John 4:17 says it best:

"As He is, so are we in this world."

Through His death and resurrection, Jesus solidified His victory over the devil and all of hell. He obtained authority and dominion over satan in every area of life. At the cross, Jesus established our superiority on this Earth, and He has never given it up. The Bible declares that the Name of Jesus is above every name that is named, and that God has put all things under His feet. The Bible also says we have been seated with Him in Heavenly places. Hallelujah, we don't have to lie prey to the enemy and his tricks!

At the root, every attack from the enemy is an attack on our identity. He comes to test us and to see if we really believe what God has spoken over us. Will we accept God's will for our lives, or settle for something less?

The Bible frames it like this in 1 Peter 5:8.

*"Be sober, be vigilant; because your adversary the devil walks about **like** a roaring lion, seeking whom he **may** devour"* (emphasis mine)

While the devil likes to make himself appear scary and powerful, I can assure you he is not. He's done a great job of portraying himself to be equal to God, or, at the very least, god-like. However, in reality, it's impossible to make him look small enough. Jesus completely whipped and stripped the enemy. You can't get more insignificant than satan is in his present state. *"The righteous are as bold as a lion"* (Proverbs 28:1), the enemy is not. The devil walks around impersonating the child of God and pretending to have the same authority. It's all an act. He's a fraud and a pathetic one at that.

In the last chapter, we talked a lot about the robe the Prodigal Son got from his father, but he also gave him a ring. In Middle Eastern culture at that time, the giving of a father's ring signified that the recipient had the authority to act and make deals in the father's name. In other words, after receiving his father's ring, the Prodigal Son became an agent of his father's business. Whenever he made a transaction, it carried the same weight as if the father had made the deal himself.

This story is a beautiful parallel of what we experience today as Children of God. When we accept Jesus as our Lord and Savior, we also receive His authority. It's as if the Heavenly Father gives us His ring, and we are now able to make commands in the Name of Jesus, to enforce the defeat of hell on this Earth. But authority only functions if you know you have it. Even if you truly have rightful authority in an area, but act as if you don't, it's not going to do you any good. Once again, this all goes back to our identity in Christ. Do we know who we are in Him? Do we know what we have access to in Him? If not, we probably won't ever enjoy the benefits. It's easy for us to look at our current situation and think that it defines us. In fact, if we choose to derive our identity from natural circumstances, we'll always find ourselves stuck there. We've all fallen prey to that sort of thinking at some point in our lives, but, trust me, my friend, the Lord has better for us than that. We need to avoid the victim mentality trap and be wary of attaching our identity to how we may feel at a given moment. That's one of the quickest ways to embrace pity rather than power.

The Lord spoke to me on this subject several years ago. He said, "Self-pity is the enemy of victory." Pity, at its root, is nothing more than us getting stuck in a victim mentality. The Enemy would love nothing more than for us to keep playing the part of a victim for our entire life, and he's always happy to help.

He'll offer us subtle suggestions, hoping all the while that he can get us to doubt who we are in Christ. He'll remind us of all the things we can't do, all the things God won't do, and all the reasons why we should blame our natural circumstances. These are all lies, mind you, but he has an insidious way of making them sound convincing.

These attacks of the enemy remind me of the story of Gideon. For those of you unfamiliar with the story, Gideon was an Old Testament Israelite surrounded by less than favorable conditions, and those outside conditions eventually affected his inside condition. Gideon and his tribe were besieged by an enemy nation, the Midianites, and things showed no signs of improving. In Judges 6:12-16, we see this play out when Gideon speaks with an Angel of the Lord.

"And the Angel of the Lord appeared to him [Gideon], and said to him, 'The Lord is with you, you mighty man of valor!' Gideon said to Him, 'O my lord, if the Lord is with us, why then has all this happened to us? And where are all His miracles which our fathers told us about, saying, 'Did not the Lord bring us up from Egypt?' But now the Lord has forsaken us and delivered us into the hands of the Midianites.' Then the Lord turned to him and said, 'Go in this might of yours, and you shall save Israel from the hand of the Midianites. Have I not sent you?' So he said to Him, 'O my Lord, how can I save Israel? Indeed my clan is the weakest in Manasseh, and I am the least in my father's house.' And the Lord said to him, 'Surely I will be with you, and you shall defeat the Midianites as one man.'"

The angel of the Lord did not come to tell Gideon where he was, but rather to call him out to a higher place that God had prepared for him. The Angel of the Lord wanted Gideon to walk in the strength God had placed *in* him, rather than fall victim to the weaknesses of the things taking place *around* him. The Angel purposely didn't address Gideon according to his present situation, and this clearly frustrated Gideon. All Gideon could see were the issues at hand, saying, "God, where are you? Why is this happening? Where are the miracles I've heard you do for others? I guess there's nothing left for us except defeat and death." He accepted that his present situation must be a permanent condition. Gideon focused on the weaknesses of his flesh and allowed despair and weakness to deplete him of his hope. His response was essentially "I'm the weakest member of the weakest family in a weak nation. I'm the weakest of the weakest!"

And right there in the middle of his complaining, the Angel of the Lord gives a rather puzzling response. The Lord's messenger calls Gideon mighty and informs him that he will be used to save Israel. Huh? At this point, Gideon seems like the least likely candidate to play the role of hero in this story, but there's one critical detail that Gideon initially failed to see. Specifically, the Lord will surely be with him. Once God entered the equation, what Gideon was once enslaved to was now destined for defeat. With the Lord by his side, Gideon could now rise up and become who God had declared him to be— a mighty man of valor!

And this transformation took place quickly. Before Judges chapter 6 was over, we see a whole new Gideon walking with a new strength given by God. Seemingly out of nowhere, Gideon gets up the courage to destroy a pagan altar. Right after this, in chapter 7, we see him rallying the troops and preparing for battle. All this is from the guy who God initially found hiding and whining in his shed.

Gideon started with an Army of several thousand men, an already slim force for the task at hand, but the Lord decided to reduce that number to a mere 300 warriors. Yet with those 300 hundred men, under the anointed wisdom and might of God, Gideon defeated the Midianites single-handedly.

Like Gideon, you may be facing a seemingly insurmountable obstacle today, and, also like Gideon, you may be feeling far too weak for the task at hand. My friend, I have good news for you. God has already called you to be a champion in Jesus! What He did for Gideon, He will most certainly do for you.
Whatever comes at you one way will be scattered and flee from you seven ways (Deuteronomy 28:7). And there is ample Scripture to back this up:

Psalm 34:19 tells us *"Many are the afflictions of the righteous, but the Lord delivers him out of them all."*

Isaiah 54:17 promises that *"'No weapon formed against you shall prosper, And every tongue which rises against you in judgment You shall condemn. This is the heritage of the servants of the Lord, And their righteousness is from Me,' Says the Lord."*

Proverbs 28:1 declares, *"The wicked flee when no one pursues, but the righteous are bold as a lion."*

Victory is your heritage. Prospering is your portion. Conquering is your birthright in Christ. Whatever weapon the devil is threatening you with is destined to fail. You're *"**always** caused to triumph in Christ Jesus"* (2

Corinthians 2:14a, emphasis mine). You're not a failure, you're a prevailer in Jesus! You don't have to stay down one more day. You can rise up now and walk in victory! Stand in the Truth of God's Word and you won't slip back into the enemy's traps. No matter how subtle the trick, you'll be able to resist him by the power of the Holy Spirit.

One major tactic the enemy will use to try and keep you in bondage is comparison. Listen, we've all been there. Comparison is a vicious cycle. It breeds doubt about who God has created us to be, and, if left unchecked, that doubt will always lead to more comparison. When you're constantly comparing yourself to others, it will rob you of the specific gifts and special anointings God has placed inside of you. As the cycle continues, it can quickly kill your confidence, kill your courage, and rob you of your joy and peace.

Comparison is the prison where destinies go to die. Oftentimes, our obsession with comparison is rooted in wrong thinking. Namely, we see ourselves as incomplete or not enough. This soon puts us on the merry-go-round, constantly comparing ourselves with those around us. We'll compare our looks, our smarts, our connections, our family, our job, our personality, and even our spouse. If God has blessed us with it, we can find a way to ruin it with comparison. There's no limit to the things the enemy will try and get us to offer up on the altar of comparison.

I've noticed that, in my own life, the areas where I allow comparison to fester usually wind up filled with bondage. All my comparison does is put me in a box, and, ultimately, it puts God in a box. Comparison is one of the easiest ways we limit the grace of God in our lives. And who on Earth would want to do that?

The devil, actually. The devil is constantly wanting you to do that. He will use comparison to belittle you, to belittle the gifts God has placed in you, and to attack the foundation of your identity. In our constant-comparison world, this can manifest in all sorts of ways- even with something as small as a personality test. Even with things like their personality. I've seen it with my own eyes. Someone will take a personality test, compare their score with those around them or what they read on the internet, and pretty soon they've created strict guidelines for how God can and cannot use them. They rewrite the plans of the Almighty based on a personality test. That they found on the internet. For free. My friend, we have to reevaluate which voices are allowed to carry weight in our lives! Our personality isn't what's holding us back, our perspective is. There's no quiz or expert on Earth that can fully understand the intricacies of how God created each one of us. God has blessed us all with so many unique giftings. Some are ready to be used for His glory from the get-go, while others take time to be honed. But, with the help of God's Spirit inside of you, you can master your personality to perform at the supernatural level that God intended. I'm not saying I'm against personality tests. What I am saying is don't limit what God can do through you based on some man-made quiz.

Friend, let me encourage you for a moment. Because of Jesus, we don't have to look at obstacles or perceived shortcomings in our lives with a victim mentality. We can view them as our next testimony, our next opportunity for victory.

This all ties back to what we discussed earlier in Numbers 13 when the Israelites sent twelve spies to vet the Promised Land. Ten of them came back with a negative report. Only two of them, Joshua and Caleb, came back with a good report. They all looked at the same territory, so their differences were purely a matter of perspective.

While the ten negative spies were pontificating all the reasons why the Israelites can't possibly follow God's command and take their Promised Land, Caleb interrupted with a very different viewpoint: "We are well able! Let us go up at once to possess the land." Joshua also hopped in and the two got so passionate about it that they tore their clothes! Joshua called the giants in the land nothing but "bread" for the Israelites, and he said the enemies would be nourishment for the people of Israel. Now, *that's* the mentality of victory!

The ten then responded, "We are not able." They'd go on to say that "they [the Israelites] were grasshoppers in their own sight and so we are in theirs [the inhabitants of the Promised Land]."

I've always thought this last statement was interesting. Think about it, how did they know the giants and all the inhabitants of the land saw them as "grasshoppers?" Did they ask them? Did they conduct interviews with their enemies to see how they viewed them? Was there a straw poll taken? Or was that response based solely on projection, specifically that the Israelites only believed their enemies saw them as incapable because that's how they saw themselves? History would go on to prove it was the latter.

And, in the end, both Caleb, Joshua, and all the rest of the Israelites got exactly what they believed. Caleb and Joshua believed they were able to possess the land, so they did. The other ten and a whole generation who followed them believed they were not able to possess the land, so they didn't.

Fast forward forty-five years, Joshua and Caleb were the only ones still alive from the previous generation. And they weren't just surviving, they were in peak shape. Caleb was 85 years old and still ready to go to war! It was at this point in his life that Caleb uttered the now famous rallying cry, "Give me this mountain!" before proceeding to thoroughly beat back the enemies of Israel (Joshua 14:12 NKJV). Even at 85 years old, his attitude was that of a victor, a champion ready to claim his inheritance! What was Caleb's secret? Later in the book of Numbers, the Lord says of Caleb that "He has a different spirit." (Numbers 14:24) In Hebrew, that word translated as "spirit" literally means an attitude or mentality. The attitude and mentality of Joshua and Caleb were not that of their grasshopper friends. They didn't see themselves as helpless victims awaiting defeat. Quite the opposite, both Joshua and Caleb were ready for battle knowing that, for them, victory was inevitable because the Lord was with them.

My friend, just like those Old Testament heroes, victory is inevitable for you today because the Lord is with you. Not only that, you can expect even better things because after what Jesus accomplished on the cross, not only is the Lord with you, but He's also *in* you! This is not a season of breaking down, it's a season of breaking through! Amen!

"Well, Pastor Jonathan," you may say, "God works in mysterious ways. He is sovereign and He is in control." Let's not blame God for our lack of faith and boldness to receive what He's already given. A great man of God, John Wesley, said it like this "It seems God can do nothing for mankind except a man asks Him." This is such a powerful perspective and one that got John Wesely in quite a bit of trouble back in his day. While I understand the sentiment behind the idea that God is in complete control of every single thing that happens here on Earth, ultimately that is not supported by what we see in Scripture, and it honestly takes away our need for faith. That way of thinking brings us to a place where we surrender our authority in Christ because whatever is going to happen will happen. *Que sera, sera.* If God wants to do it, He will, if He doesn't, He won't, and we're all just along for the ride. However, if we put our faith in the finished work of Christ, that kind of belief will stir us up to go after all God has made available to us.

My friend, my heart's desire for you is for you to dominate and overcome in *this* life through our Lord Jesus. I hate the devil and I hate the oppression he tries to place on humanity! But I thank God all the more for the victory He won for us at the cross! We don't have to remain a slave to the enemy and his works. We've been set free forever by the blood of Jesus! I urge you to work on changing your mindset, or "spirit," towards these things so that you can walk in God's blessings more and more. Begin to enjoy His freedom! We are not sitting ducks waiting for something bad to happen to us. The other shoe is not going to drop. You're a roaring lion with the ability to live in the goodness of God. Let your lion out today! Let the Spirit of God inside of you stir you up to stand in faith today. You're not going under, you're going over. You are the head and not the tail. You are above and never beneath. God's favor and blessing rests on your life. Today is a new day of victory for you and your family. The reign of tyranny the devil has had over you is officially over. God has given you the authority and power to rule and reign in this life. Take it, use it, and live the life of an overcomer in Jesus' name!

Chapter 9: Abide in Him

"I am a true sprouting vine, and the farmer who tends the vine is my Father. He cares for the branches connected to me by lifting and propping up the fruitless branches and pruning every fruitful branch to yield a greater harvest. The words I have spoken over you have already cleansed you. So you must remain in life-union with Me, for I remain in life-union with you. For as a branch severed from the vine will not bear fruit, so your life will be fruitless unless you live your life intimately joined to mine. I am the sprouting vine and you're my branches. As you live in union with Me as your source, fruitfulness will stream from within you—but when you live separated from Me you are powerless."

John 15:1-5 TPT

I love the simplicity with which Jesus describes the good life— a life of simply abiding in Him. This Truth is the key to living a fruitful life. When we choose to abide in Christ, listen to His word, and renew our minds to the truths of Scripture, we begin to grow, bloom, and flourish. It's really not that complicated, though some theologians try to make it so. To put it very plainly, living outside of Jesus is pointless, fruitless, and restless. Living inside of Jesus is purposeful, fruitful, and peaceful. Living a life in communion with Christ will cause you to remain *full*. Full of life, full of joy, and full of peace. He's our safe place.

The Bible says *"The Name of the Lord is a strong tower; the righteous runs **into** it and is safe"*
Proverbs 18:10 ESV (emphasis mine)

Steadfast and unshakable security can be found only in Him. Even in the midst of storms and chaos, we can always find safe refuge in Jesus. There is a beautiful illustration of this principle hidden in an Old Testament story—Noah and the ark. I'm going to go out on a limb and assume that if you grew up in America, you're acquainted with the story. God instructed Noah to build an ark because a flood was coming. For forty days while the rain continued to pour down and flood waters surged across the Earth, Noah and his family were safe and sound inside the ark. Sound familiar? Good.

The Old Testament ark was a type and shadow of our New Testament Jesus. He's our shelter from the storm, our shade in the heat, our fortress when we feel weary. When you feel weak, He'll be your strength. No matter what's going on around you, you and your family can stay safe by remaining in Him. We can decide that as for us and our house, we'll stay in the ark, we'll abide in Jesus.

Where we abide is our choice. We must be careful not to slide back into the pain and regret of abiding in our past. The enemy will use anything and everything to try and move us off our present position in Christ. In my ministry experience, one area I often see the devil exploit is past hurt. He'll try to use the pain from our childhood or trauma from our past to blind us to the grace of Jesus in the present.

My friend, hear this Word from the Lord for you, pain and trauma are not your masters. I know the pain is real. I know the hurt cut deep. But this only makes the sacrifice of Jesus all the more wonderful. Our precious Jesus bore the full brunt of this suffering on the cross at Calvary! Because of Him, we don't have to stay prisoners to our past. We do not need to pretend the trauma never happened, but because of Jesus, we can overcome it once and for all. Past trauma may have been a dark period in your life, but it doesn't have to be your permanent address.

The enemy loves to cause and exploit past hurts because he knows these things will hold us back in life. They will limit our relationships and hinder our intimacy with the Lord and the people He's placed in our lives. If past hurt makes us afraid to open up, our connections with people will be surface level at best. But instead of choosing to abide in the pain, we can abide in the Healer of all pain. The Bible says Jesus is near to the broken-hearted and binds up those broken pieces to make you whole again.

When the famous line in Psalm 23:3 says, "He restores my soul," the Hebrew word is literally speaking of our mind, will, and emotions. The Lord wants to heal whatever has left your mind in chaos and caused your emotions to spin out of control. Mental oppression and mental illness don't have to be lifelong ailments. The same Jesus who heals the body heals the mind, and God's heart for all of us is to live restored, redeemed, and restful in His love for us.

Abide in Him, abide in His love. Those are the words ringing in my heart for God's Church today. In these last days you and I live in, abiding with the Master must be a priority. The Bible says that times of refreshing come from the presence of the Lord. How can we abide in Him? By worshiping Him. Taking time to acknowledge His presence in your life and the life you have through Him. You can take time to abide in His presence by praying in the Spirit. You can be refreshed by remaining in His Word. You can even abide in His love by investing in the relationships and friendships with people He's placed in your life. God hasn't made it difficult to remain in Him. Quite the opposite, you can find His Spirit and His presence with you wherever you may go. I love the closing lines of John 15:5 TPT that so beautifully illustrates this:

"As you live in union with Me as your source, fruitfulness will stream from within you—but when you live separated from Me you are powerless."

I often wonder how much of our time, energy, money, and sanity we pour into the futile mission of trying to be fruitful apart from Him. We are powerless by ourselves to bear fruit. Self-reliance and self-dependence always lead us to frustration. It's vital that we stay dependent on and connected to the Lord for our growth and supply.

The Bible says in Proverbs 10:22, *"The Blessing of the Lord makes one rich, and He adds no sorrow with it."* The word sorrow in Hebrew literally means "pain, hurt, toil, labor, or hardship." I believe this verse shows us that, because Jesus has put us permanently under the blessing, we can live a fruitful and prosperous life rather than toiling with laborious effort just to scrape by.

Don't get me wrong, there are a lot of ways to get money. But there's only one way that involves no pain or sorrow. There are many ways to get healed, but only one way to be whole. There are a number of ways to appear fruitful, but only one that brings lasting results without frustration. This *One Way* I'm talking about is Jesus. He is where true wholeness and prosperity and fruitfulness can be found. He is the source of all good things in our lives. This doesn't mean that we won't face challenges and obstacles on this Earth. Believe me, you will.[8] However, what it does mean is that, in the midst of these tribulations, we're connected to an endless source of strength. Jesus gives us the power to overcome, and, in Him, there's true freedom from all bondage. And I mean *all.* There's no area in our lives that His grace can't transform.

---

[8] Editor concurs.

In the previous chapter, we talked a lot about the Children of Israel and their journey to the promised land. But for centuries before they possessed their land, they lived as slaves in Egypt. After roughly 400 years, oppression became a normal operating procedure for them. Eventually, as I'm sure most Sunday school regulars are familiar with, God sent great plagues and delivered His people from their bondage. Begrudgingly, Pharaoh set the Israelites free. For a minute. And then changed his mind and set his army after them.

When the Israelites came upon the Red Sea, with Pharaoh's army in hot pursuit, the Bible says the Israelites cried out to God in fear and said the following ridiculous statement:

"Because there were no graves in Egypt, have you taken us away to die in the wilderness? ...It would have been better for us to serve the Egyptians than that we should die in the wilderness." Exodus 14:11,14

Despite their fear and complaining, God still parted the Red Sea so the Children of Israel could walk across on dry ground.

Flash forward to the next chapter, Exodus 15, and we pick up with the Israelites having been in the wilderness for three days without water. When they finally arrived at a place known as Marah, the only water they found was bitter and undrinkable. Once again, bitter complaining ensued and God, in His mercy, made the bitter waters sweet.

This trend continued into Exodus 16, where the Children of Israel were once again complaining—this time about not having enough food. And again, the Israelites leveled ridiculous accusations against the Lord:

"Oh, that we had died by the hand of the Lord in the land of Egypt, when we sat by the pots of meat and when we ate bread to the full! For you have brought us out into this wilderness to kill this whole assembly with hunger." Exodus 16:3.

Then God, as usual, supplied their need by raining bread from Heaven.

You'd think Israel would catch on at this point, but you'd be wrong. Once again, in Exodus 17, we see them enter into another round of complaints. They were thirsty again and cried out:

"Why is it you have brought us up out of Egypt, to kill us and our children and our livestock with thirst?" Exodus 17:3

We then see God supernaturally provide water from a rock for the *second time* after He instructed Moses to strike it with his rod. Once again, God mercifully provided for an ungrateful people.

I bring these stories up to illustrate that, even after God had physically delivered them from bondage, the Israelites still had a slavery mentality. They would quickly forget the merciful nature of their God and the covenant they had with Him. I say all of this as a picture of our own fight of faith today. We must be careful not to fall into the trap of the Israelites and allow our current situation to send us back into a bondage mentality—even after we have been delivered by the Lord. We must be careful not to choose the dark familiarity of our old prisons over the sometimes-startling bright light of freedom. Stepping out of familiar territory can be scary, but new freedom is always better than past bondage. Gaining ground may be tough at times, but the battle is always worth it. Daring to possess your promised land may induce a fight, but it will always be a good one. Staying in bondage may feel safer, but it's the slow path toward death. Both choices bring with them a struggle: the former up toward inevitable victory, and the latter down to inevitable defeat. The Scripture says it best:

"At last we have freedom, for Christ has set us free! We must always cherish this truth and firmly refuse to go back into the bondage of our past" (Galatians 5:1 TPT)

We must not allow the enemy to put a yoke of slavery on us again by forcing us back into a bondage mentality. We need to keep our eyes on Jesus, and constantly remind ourselves of the precious promises in His Word. We need to remember that God is for us, not against us. That He is our Good Shepherd, always leading and always providing. When the enemy screams in our ears that we have been forsaken, we need to do the exact opposite of the Israelites in Exodus, and instead choose to believe the Word of the Lord rather than our present circumstances. We can refuse to return to bondage and instead opt to stand firm in the freedom Christ has given us. God desires for us to live in liberty—we don't have to act like slaves when God has made us sons.

The devil desires for us to waste time trying to earn something we already have in Christ. He'll work tirelessly to make us feel as though we're incomplete or that we must work for God to earn His acceptance. My friend, more than anything in this world, God desires a relationship with us. He would rather spend five minutes communing with us than spend five weeks burning ourselves out attempting to earn His seal of approval.

My heartfelt prayer is that we would truly know God loves us! He passionately desires to reveal His acceptance and approval to us. I believe it saddens the heart of our Father when His own kids feel they owe Him a debt, a debt that has already been paid by Jesus at the cross. Right now, as we stand today, we can abide in the very presence of God without a sense of guilt, inferiority or shame. The only things that await us in His presence are unconditional love and endless grace.

Don't live your life working *for* God with a distant relationship. Let's stay *with* Him, work with Him, and live every day with an intimate knowledge of His presence surrounding us. We can live ever aware of the position and promises we have in Christ, that Heaven is our inheritance and God has made it available for us to walk in today.

Throughout this book, we've talked a lot about the story of the Prodigal Son, but that story is actually about two sons, not just one. Notice how the father's oldest son acted when his prodigal brother returned:

"Now his older son was in the field. And as he came and drew near to the house, he heard music and dancing. So, he called one of the servants and asked what these things meant. And he said to him, 'Your brother has come, and because he has received him safe and sound, your father has killed the fatted calf.'

*"But he was angry and would not go in. Therefore his father came out and pleaded with him. So he answered and said to his father, 'Lo, these many years I have been **serving** you; I never transgressed your commandment at any time; and yet you never gave me a young goat, that I might make merry with my friends. But as soon as this son of yours came, who has devoured your livelihood with harlots, you killed the fatted calf for him.'*

*"And he said to him, '**Son**, you are always with me, and all that I have is yours. It was right that we should make merry and be glad, for your brother was dead and is alive again, and was lost and is found.'"*

Luke 15:25-32 (emphasis mine)

The older son approached his father more like an employee rather than a member of the family. According to his father, the older brother could have enjoyed a party and partook of the benefits of sonship at any time, yet he chose to toil away in the fields like a common laborer. In essence, he was trying to earn something he already had. He decided rather than abiding with his father, he'd work as a slave.

Please don't misunderstand me, I am a firm believer in the idea that we should serve God, but there's a big difference between working *for* the Kingdom and working *in* the Kingdom. You don't have to act like an employee when you're an owner. More than anything, the father in this parable simply wanted to just be with his sons. That's made clear by his interactions with his kids: first how he welcomed the prodigal son home, and then in the way, he pleaded with his oldest son to join the celebration. A loving dad who just wanted his kids to abide with him—what an image of our Heavenly Father!

Friend, more than what you're called to do, remember you're called *to Him* first. Our top priority is to *be* not to *do.* It's easy for us to get so caught up in serving Jesus that we forget to just be with Him.

We see a perfect example of this in Luke 10:38-42 when Jesus visits the home of his friends Mary and Martha. As the story progresses, we see two very distinct pictures of how the sisters chose to welcome

Jesus into their home. Mary chose to sit at His feet and hear His Word. Martha decided that serving Jesus should be her top priority and she quickly became agitated with Mary for her lack of help. In fact, Martha gets so irritated that she interrupts Jesus in the middle of his conversation and demands that He orders Mary to help with the serving. The Lord's reaction would surprise a lot of religious-minded folks, even today. Jesus looked lovingly at Martha and said:

*"Martha, Martha, you are worried and troubled about many things. But one thing is **needed,** and Mary has chosen that good part which will not be taken away from her"* Luke 10:41-42 (emphasis mine).

Jesus is instructing Martha and, consequently, instructing us that only one thing is needed in our lives—and that's to abide in Him. Crazy as it may sound, that is the beautifully simple Truth of the Gospel. It may seem elementary and overly simplified, but it remains the heart of our Heavenly Father toward His children. His delight is in us and our fellowship with Him. He craves family relationships. He cares about who we are, not just what we can perform.

And, just like every other Truth in Scripture, this all comes back to Jesus. He paid the price for our salvation at the cross just so we could be welcomed into the presence of God once again. Under the Old Testament Mosaic Law, God's presence was confined to a single place: the Holy of Holies. Only the High Priest was allowed to enter into the Holy of Holies, and even then only on the rarest of occasions and with extreme caution. This was not just difficult for man; it was difficult for God. The Lord, who is Love Himself, had to hide His presence from the creation He loved so much. God is altogether righteous and just, so He separated from mankind until sin could be defeated—but he certainly didn't enjoy it.

This is what makes the work of Jesus even more beautiful! In the same passage, we see Him give up His life on the cross to pay the price for our sins, the very next thing we see is the temple veil that protected the Holy of Holies—separating God from His people—ripping in half from the top to the bottom. At the first possible moment, God threw open the door for all mankind to freely abide in His presence once again. But the Lord didn't only want the veil torn so we could come in, He wanted to get *out* and dwell inside each of us believers!

My dear friend, choosing to abide constantly in Him will mean the difference between living full or living depleted. Frankly, it is the determining factor in how fruitful and full our lives become. We need to shift our mindset away from thinking that God is distant, some disinterested being far out in the cosmos. Instead, we need to focus on becoming God-inside-minded. For believers, God is not just *out there*, He's dwelling *in here*—inside us! Jesus said it Himself that He would never leave us nor forsake us.

Abiding in Him is abiding in victory. Abiding in Him is abiding in healing. Abiding in Him is abiding in prosperity. Abiding in Him is abiding in breakthrough. Allow the secret place of the Most High God to become your dwelling place and watch and enjoy the supernatural change that takes place in your life. Allow the revelation of Jesus being your Good Shepherd to wash over your soul. A good shepherd knows his sheep, stays with his sheep, leads his sheep, protects his sheep, values his sheep, and loves his sheep. Believe in His goodness. Trust in His ability to be your source of life and strength. From now on, let your confession testify not of your own weakness, but instead of your victorious position in Christ. Let your heart rejoice in your newfound identity in Jesus.

Friend, let's make this confession of faith together today, "Surely my Shepherd cares for me. Surely my Shepherd calls me by name. Surely my Shepherd leads me out of bondage. Surely my Shepherd leads me by the still waters. Surely my Shepherd leads me to the green pastures. Surely my Shepherd makes me whole. Surely my Shepherd walks with me all the days of my life."

Throughout this book, we've discussed several common strategies of the enemy to try and give you an "identity crisis." All these tactics basically have the same end goal: getting you to see yourself outside of Christ, separated away from your loving source of supply. Friend, don't let this happen to you. Stand firm against the devil's lies! Cast down those thoughts that are contrary to the Truth of God's Word! Remember your unshakable position in Christ and lay hold of all the good possessions He has in store for you. Allow the beauty of God's Word, and nothing else, to define you.

Make it a priority every day to acknowledge the victorious position you have in Jesus. And always remember that your new standing before God isn't temporary, it's eternal. We can access our Heavenly inheritance today, at any time and in any place. Through Jesus, we can live above a culture of deteriorating mental health, we can rise above the "new normal" and enjoy a life full of joy, peace, and mental soundness.

We're a part of God's Kingdom. Greater is He that is in us than anything that will ever come against us. Now is not the time for us believers to shrink back in fear, now is the time to take ground for Heaven! Beloved, boldly possess your Promised Land by faith! Go after everything God has for you! You can be who He said you are. You can do what He said you can do. You can have what He says you can have. Don't settle. Wake up every day with the revelation of your identity in Christ and live it out! Keep your head up, your heart guarded, your mind renewed, your faith extended, and your life connected to our wonderful Jesus.

Acknowledgments:

To my Wonderful Lord Jesus, thank You for Your revelation, grace, and guidance in writing this book. I pray every word brings You honor and glory.

To my Beautiful Wife, Katie, thank you for your encouragement, love, and support. Your heart for people and for Jesus is inspiring. Thank you for always standing by my side and pushing me to follow Jesus. And thank you for always giving me such great hugs!

To my amazing Parents, Pastors Tony and Denise. Thank you for teaching me about Jesus and showing me how to trust Him with my whole heart. You taught me faith, you taught me the Word, and you helped guide me in ministry. Thank you both from the bottom of my heart!

To my incredible Mother and Father in love, Gary and Kimberly Waters. You both have always shown unhesitant support for me, my life, and this project. I count myself truly blessed to call you my family! I love you both!

To my Siblings, all of you mean so much to me! Thank you for always being in my corner and showing relentless support in all God leads me to do. I love all of you so much!

To Jonathan Lauria, my book editor and friend, I am indebted to you for your passionate contribution to this project. I'll live forever grateful for you.

To Cowan Creative, for making me and the book graphics look fantastic!

To all my friends who encouraged me while writing this book. Each of you holds a special place in my heart and I thank God for blessing me with such great faith friends!

Salvation Prayer

If you would like to receive Jesus and His free gift of
salvation, please pray this prayer with me:

Lord Jesus, thank you for loving me! Thank you for
shedding your blood for my redemption and giving Your
life for my salvation. I believe God raised You from the
dead and that You are alive today. I declare that You are
my Lord and Savior. Thank you that I am forgiven and
have been accepted in Your Beloved family. Thank you
for making my heart Your home, for giving me eternal
life, and for filling me with Your joy and peace. In Jesus'
name. Amen!

About the Author

Jonathan Cowan is a licensed and ordained minister and a preacher of the Gospel of Grace. He and his wife, Katie currently serve on the Pastoral Staff at Church 316 in Athens, Ga. They separately help to lead Cowan Ministries. Their passion is to help people find out their true identity in Jesus and help them walk out God's perfect plan for their lives.

Jonathan first felt the call to ministry at the young age of seven years old. Since then, he has dedicated his life to studying and learning all he can about God's Word and the truth about who we are in Him. His heart's desire is to help bring a greater revelation of what it truly means to live a life free from sin, shame, guilt, and fear through the finished work of Jesus!

His writing style, much like his speaking style, is dynamic with an anointing to boldly proclaim the truth found in God's Word.

Please visit cowanministries.org for additional resources. You can also follow him @jonathancowan on Facebook and Instagram, and subscribe to his YouTube channel for messages, podcasts, and more.